Gary Jones

New Zealand

Contents

1

Introduction

New Zealand may be on the other side of the world and, depending on where you are departing from, can take up to 14 hours to reach it with a direct flight, but the island nation is a popular tourist destination. When you arrive in New Zealand, its stunning natural beauty, unique culture and an amazing array of attractions will amaze you.

Where is New Zealand?

New Zealand is situated in the Pacific Ocean, around 900 miles (or 1500 kilometers southeast of Australia and around 600 miles south of

Fiji.

New Zealand Map
https://goo.gl/maps/oAuJCWqj4T42

New Zealand Geography

New Zealand covers an area of around 103,500 square miles or 268,000 square kilometers, which is roughly the same area as the state of Colorado in the United States. It consists of two main islands – named the North Island and the South Island – as well as numerous other islands. Both the North and South Islands feature their own distinctive landscapes, making them unique.

New Zealand Plants and Animals

New Zealand was one of the oldest parts of the Gondwanan supercontinent, which broke off roughly around 80 million years ago. Because of this, New Zealand was able to develop animal and plant-life, which is unique to these islands, in addition to being blessedly free from snakes and other predatory animals. The kiwi is the national bird, a small nocturnal flightless bird whose native home is in the forests.

Before the Europeans arrived in the 19th century, forests spread across the country, much of which has now been cut down in order for towns and settlements to be established. However, there are a number of trees and other plants that have been able to escape this fate, including the Kauri Trees on the North Island and the beech trees on the South Island. Other old trees are protected and are part of the country's National Parks.

New Zealand People

Commonly referred to as 'kiwis', the people of New Zealand are exceptionally friendly and welcome all who come to visit their beautiful country. There are around 4.4 million people living in New Zealand, which is quite low when compared to other countries, but the ethnic groups are many. Before the Europeans came and settled in New Zealand, the original inhabitants living here were the Maori people who currently make up around 15% of the total population. The descendants of the Europeans, or Caucasians, make up around 70%, and the other 15% is made up of Asians and Pacific Islanders.

New Zealand Language and Culture

The two official languages of New Zealand are English and Maori. As a result of being inhabited by so many people, New Zealand is home to many cultures, including the original Maori culture.

2

History

New Zealand is a young country in regards to both geography and human history and was the last inhabitable place discovered by humans.

The Maori

The ancestors of the Maori were the first people to arrive in New Zealand. Anthropologists and archaeologists believe that the Maori ancestors arrived from Polynesia sometime between 1200 and 1300 CE, discovering the islands after traveling across the ocean, steering their vessels by the stars at night. Kupe is generally accredited the discovery of New Zealand.

The Europeans

The first European to set foot on New Zealand was a Dutch explorer named Abel Tasman who arrived in 1642, and it was a Dutch mapmaker who first referred to the country as Nieuw Zeeland. The second European to arrive in New Zealand was 127 years later. Captain James Coo arrived in 1769, the first voyage out of three to this area.

After this time, Europeans started to arrive more frequently, typically those who hunted whales and seals and then traders. In the early 19th century, the British were experiencing pressure to take control of the amount of mayhem and crime which was abundant throughout the islands in addition to beating the French, who were also debating as to whether to make New Zealand a colony for themselves.

On the 6th February 1840, the first governor of New Zealand, William Hobson, summoned the Maori chiefs to Waitangi where they were asked to sign a treaty with the British Empire. This treaty traveled all around the islands and was signed by over 500 Maori chiefs.

Conflict and Development

The Maori experience strong pressure for decades by the Europeans to sell their land. As a consequence, the Maori and the Europeans found themselves in a civil war in the 1860s and the next two decades found a high percentage of Maori land on the North Island either confiscated or purchased.

On the South Island, however, the people experienced a different lifestyle. Sheep farming developed greatly, and Canterbury prospered into the richest province. In the mid-19th century, gold was uncovered in Otago and then the West Coast the following decade, allowing

Dunedin to become the biggest town in the region.

During the 1870s, railways were established to help the influx of British people settle in New Zealand. In 1882, the first shipment of frozen meat from New Zealand arrived in Britain, thus allowing the export of meat, butter, and cheese to begin. Even today, New Zealand lamb is still a major stable of British households. As a result, much of the forests that covered New Zealand were cut down, allowing more farmland to be created.

Changes in Social Life and War

New Zealand was the first country in the world in 1893 which gave women the legal right to vote, as well as being the first country to offer state pensions and workers' housing.

In 1899, New Zealand provided the British Empire with troops who joined in the South African "Boer" War. New Zealand was offered the chance to join the Australian Federation in 1901 but became an independent territory in 1907.

During World War One, New Zealand sent their own troops, many of whom perished. The landing at Gallipoli in 1915 brought about the establishment of the ANZAC, otherwise known as the Australian and New Zealand Army Corps. On the 25th April each year, the ANZAC Day is celebrated.

Joining the Allies during World War Two, New Zealand sent many troops to help, but when Singapore fell, the country soon began to have doubts about the British strength. When their troops fought against the Japanese in the Pacific, the Americans helped the New Zealanders.

Late 20th Century

During the 1950s, America encouraged New Zealand to fight in the Korean War and even though the move wasn't popular, they fought in the Vietnam War the following decade.

Until the early 1970s, New Zealand had exported its products mainly to Britain but in 1973, the United Kingdom joined the European Economic Community, which forced New Zealand into exporting its products to other countries to make up for the loss.

3

Useful Information You Need to Know

New Zealand is a beautiful country and quite easy to get around to see everything, but unless you have been there before, it is best to understand certain things to make your visit more pleasurable.

Climate

In the topmost north of the country, the weather is subtropical during the summer months while the mountainous areas of the South Island can plunge to –10°C (14°F) during the colder months. However, since the coast is never too far away, the temperature stays mild all the year through.

The temperature gets colder the further south you go. January and February are the best times to visit, as the temperature is the warmest, with July actually being the coldest. The summer months sees the temperatures rise to 20 – 30°C or 70 – 90°F whereas the average temperature in winter is around 10 – 15°C or 50 – 60°F.

Rain

New Zealand is known for its beautiful scenery but is also quite renowned for its rainy weather through the year. The average rainfall increases during the winter months in the north and central areas but in the southern areas of the country the winter period has the least amount of rain. Because of the high amount of rainfall, the country is great for farming.

Snow

Snow generally falls in New Zealand between June and October, although there are other times when it can appear. The majority of the snow occurs during the high, mountainous altitudes, as well as inland areas such as Canterbury and Otago.

New Zealand Emergency Phone Number: **111**

New Zealand Emergency Website
https://www.newzealandnow.govt.nz/living-in-nz
/safety/emergency-services

Money

The currency in New Zealand is the New Zealand Dollar (NZ$), but credit cards can be used throughout the country, with Visa and MasterCard being the most popular. International visitors can bring in as much foreign money as they want but if you bring more than NZ$10,000 in or out of the country, then you must fill out a Border Cash Report. You can exchange foreign currency at the many Bureau de Change kiosks located in the cities and airports, as well as banks and many hotels.

Border Cash Report Website 1
https://www.aucklandairport.co.nz/information/arriving-from-overseas/boarder-processing-requirements
Border Cash Report Website 2
http://www.customs.govt.nz/Pages/default.aspx

Tipping and Service Charges

It is not necessary to tip in New Zealand, even in bars and restaurants, but you can tip if your server has been good. A service charge is not added to bills in hotels or restaurants.

Goods and Services Tax

A 15% Goods and Service Tax (GST) is added to every goods and services in New Zealand, but this is included in the displayed price. This tax cannot be claimed back by international visitors but it is omitted from the price of big purchases when they are shipped overseas to the guest's home.

4

Getting To and Around New Zealand

Airports

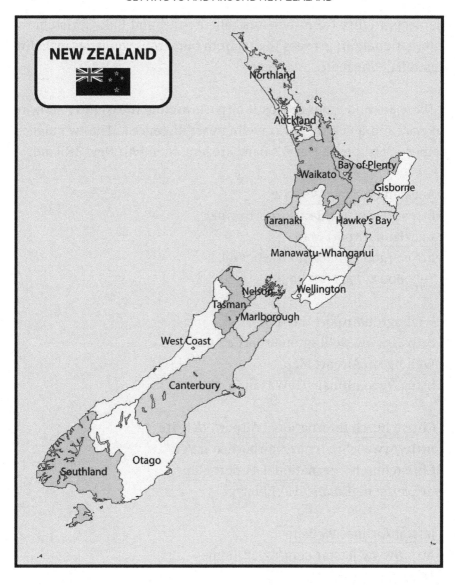

New Zealand has a number of airports serving international and domestic flights. Auckland Airport is the largest and busiest airport, connecting with many cities around the world. Wellington Airport connects flights from four Australian cities and Fiji; Christchurch International Airport sees flights from numerous countries including Australia, Singapore, and Japan.

There are numerous domestic airports around the country allowing an easy and quick way of traveling vast distances. The two biggest domestic airlines in New Zealand are Jetstar and Air New Zealand.

Auckland Airport Website
https://www.aucklandairport.co.nz/
Auckland Airport Map
https://goo.gl/maps/FA0AQ12CejL2
Tel:0800247767 (24 hours)

Wellington Airport Website
https://www.wellingtonairport.co.nz/
Wellington Airport Map
https://goo.gl/maps/TyW43ajjX672

Christchurch International Airport Website
http://www.christchurchairport.co.nz/en/
Christchurch International Airport Map
https://goo.gl/maps/dGVEJibdyyz

Jetstar Airlines Website
http://www.jetstar.com/nz/en/home
Tel:6499759426

Air New Zealand Website
http://www.airnewzealand.co.nz/domestic-fares
Tel:0800737000(Calling in NZ)
Tel:64093573000(Calling from overseas)

Driving

A great way to explore the best of New Zealand is by car, caravan or a motorhome. The first thing you should know is that cars drive on the left-hand side of the road, but this section will cover other useful things you need to be aware of before you start up your vehicle.

The terrain in New Zealand is vast and diverse. Because of this, the roads in the country can sometimes be narrow and have hard and quick turns. There are only a couple of motorways outside the key cities; many roads are single lanes and gravel roads are frequent.

Because many roads are narrow and windy, it is often the case when drivers don't realize how long it takes to get somewhere. As an example, what looks like a three-hour drive from Hokitika to Haast will actually take around four hours because the roads are so windy. This will be the case throughout the country.

The weather will affect the roads. While the day may begin sunny, by nightfall it can be rainy. As a result, the roads are often affected by the weather. Before you start your journey to anywhere, be sure that you check what the weather will be like that day and be prepared. Remember that snow can fall in the South Island in fall, winter and spring so make sure that you carry snow chains in your car. Rental companies will show you how to put them on if you have no previous experience.

Buses and Coaches

A cheaper way of exploring the country is via bus and coach. Each region has its own network of buses that span distances and a fleet of coaches that travel up and down the country. Many of the popular attractions can be reached via bus or coach.

Intercity Bus Website

http://www.intercity.co.nz/
Tel:095835780(Calling in NZ)
Tel:+6495835780(Calling from overseas)

Atomic Travel Website
http://www.atomictravel.co.nz/
Tel:+64033490697

Trains

Due to the diverse and rugged landscape, building New Zealand's railways has always been a challenge but offer a unique, and cheaper, way of seeing the country.

Rail New Zealand Website
http://www.railnewzealand.com/

5

PART 1 - NORTH ISLAND

NEW ZEALAND

The geography of the North Island is simply too beautiful for words. An amazing array of attractions, both man-made and natural, awaits all those who venture to the far north. This is the place where the political history of the country began, a region where farmlands blend seamlessly with coastlines and geothermal attractions along with the rich Maori culture.

North Island Map
https://goo.gl/maps/BwRXSpqGMEp

6

Northland and Bay of Islands

Referred to as the Winterless North, the Northland and Bay of Islands is a spectacular region well-known for its combination of sandy beaches, Kauri tree forests, gigantic sand dunes and charming islands dotted around the coastline.

Northland Map
https://goo.gl/maps/htFTJgsS58z

Bay of Islands Map
https://goo.gl/maps/fPttKHhhUz62

This region enjoys a subtropical climate through the year, which attracts thousands of visitors annually just for that reason alone. The Bay of Islands is a great place to visit. One of the best islands to visit is

Urupukapuka Island and don't miss out on the chance to visit **Tapeka Point**.

An hour's drive from here will lead you to the harbor town of **Tutukaka**, which gives you the entrance to the **Poor Knights Marine Reserve**. If you have any interest in diving, then the Poor Knights Marine Reserve is certainly one of the best places to visit.

For those interested in seeing the ancient Kauri trees, then definitely pay a visit to **Trounson Kauri Forest** or even Waipoua Forest, the latter of which boasts the Lord of the Forest (also known as Tane Mahuta), a Kauri tree which is more than 2,000 years old and stands 51 meters high.

Adrenaline junkies should make their way to **Hokianga**. Hire a boogie board, sail across the water and go sailing down the Te Paki Sand Dunes.

Urupukapuka Island Website

http://www.doc.govt.nz/parks-and-recreation
/places-to-go/northland/places/urupukapuka-island-
recreation-reserve/
Urupukapuka Island Map
https://goo.gl/maps/91VofLvRrhy

Tapeka Point Website
http://www.tapeka.com/tapeka_point.htm
Tapeka Point Map
https://goo.gl/maps/DTf44REgv9t

Tutukaka Website
http://www.tutukakacoastnz.com/
Tutukaka Map
https://goo.gl/maps/m8Cze3ZbGCR2

Poor Knights Marine Reserve Website
http://diving.co.nz/poor-knights-islands
Poor Knights Marine Reserve Map
https://goo.gl/maps/Qaghr9dPtG22

Trounson Kauri Forest Website
http://www.doc.govt.nz/parks-and-recreation/
places-to-go/northland/places
/trounson-kauri-park/
Trounson Kauri Forest Map
https://goo.gl/maps/KhvCreyg8Bo

Waipoua Forest Website
http://www.doc.govt.nz/parks-and-recreation
/places-to-go/northland/places/waipoua-forest/
Waipoua Forest Map
https://goo.gl/maps/xrsDP5XiM1A2

Hokianga Website
http://www.hokianga.co.nz/
Hokianga Map
https://goo.gl/maps/t4KMKgq789t

Te Paki Sand Dunes
https://goo.gl/maps/Q9cC5zzjGGv
Te Paki Sand Dunes
http://pukenuiholidaypark.co.nz/giant-te-paki-sand-dunes/

7

Auckland

Auckland

Auckland is the largest city in New Zealand and the principal transport center. As a major city, Auckland boasts a great amount of things to see and do, in addition to a wide variety of restaurants and accommodation for all budgets. You can spend one day wandering around the harbor area, taking in the sights, the next you can head outside the city and immerse yourself in the beauty of the rugged landscape.

Auckland Map
https://goo.gl/maps/dy2Yw5AGh3S2

Even in the middle of the city it doesn't take that long to get on the water. There are a number of tour companies that offer trips where you can get to know the local wildlife, including **marine safaris**. Perfect for children and adults alike, you can come up close with dolphins, whales, and orcas in the **Hauraki Gulf Marine Park**. Or you can simply enjoy sailing yourself if you have the necessary experience. Failing that, simply head onto a boat and relax.

Marine Safaris Website
http://www.awads.co.nz/tours--pricing.html
Marine Safaris Map
https://goo.gl/maps/YkF9KX2oLjE2

Hauraki Gulf Marine Park Website
http://www.doc.govt.nz/haurakigulfmarinepark
Hauraki Gulf Marine Park Map
https://goo.gl/maps/y8RRntinh6J2

Due to its close proximity to the ocean, there are a number of boat day trips you can enjoy. **Kayaking to Rangitoto Island** is a highly popular tour, especially at sunset, or sail on a true America's Cup yacht. For history lovers, jump on the ferry to **Devonport** where you can shop until you drop, feast on delectable culinary delights and then start exploring the World War Two tunnels and other sites at North Head.

Auckland Sea Kayaks Website
http://www.aucklandseakayaks.co.nz/auckland-kayak-tours/
sunset-kayak-tour-rangitoto-island/

Auckland Sea Kayaks Map
https://goo.gl/maps/H4kzKfWZSP22

Devonport Website
http://www.devonport.co.nz/
Devonport Map
https://goo.gl/maps/q2ZzphV1dbs
Auckland Ferry Website
https://at.govt.nz/bus-train-ferry/ferry-services/

Discover the islands of the Hauraki Gulf
The **Hauraki Gulf** is located not far from Auckland and features a wide range of natural and historical attractions, including a fantastic array of islands, each one more beautiful than the last. One particular island not to pass up on seeing is in the middle and known as **Rangitoto**. This volcanic island has black lava, making it a truly remarkable place. Hire a kayak and head towards it either at sunrise or sunset for a magical experience.

Hauraki Gulf Website
https://haurakibluecruises.co.nz/auckland-hauraki-gulf-islands-guide/
Hauraki Gulf Map
https://goo.gl/maps/Ug5wQEiQxRq

Rangitoto Island Website
http://www.doc.govt.nz/rangitoto
Rangitoto Island Map
https://goo.gl/maps/jFWXk6SEdiA2

Waiheke Island, located 30 minutes away via ferry from the center of Auckland offers visitors the chance to enjoy wine tasting and superb beaches to relax on, whilst **Motuihe Island** offers family-friendly beaches and swimming. Kawau Island's main attraction is the Mansion House, the former residence of Governor George Grey. Animal lovers will fall head over heels at the wildlife sanctuary located on **Tiritiri Matangi Island**, which houses the rare Takahe birds. And don't miss out on visiting **Great Barrier Island**, which boasts natural hot springs.

Waiheke Island Website
http://www.waiheke.co.nz/
Waiheke Island Map
https://goo.gl/maps/3CxWKbjUbZM2

Motuihe Island Website
http://www.motuihe.org.nz/
Motuihe Island Map

https://goo.gl/maps/daPEnrJa44E2

Kawau Island Website
http://www.kawauisland.org.nz/general-kawau
-information
Kawau Island Map
https://goo.gl/maps/3kLa74e3JUn

Tiritiri Matangi Island Website
http://www.tiritirimatangi.org.nz/
Tiritiri Matangi Island Map
https://goo.gl/maps/PZoAEYuZL8p

Great Barrier Island Website
http://www.thebarrier.co.nz/
Great Barrier Island Map
https://goo.gl/maps/y4oxPP5uhND2

Family Fun

New Zealand is a great place to bring children, no matter how old they are, and Auckland is certainly a family-friendly destination. Here are a few suggestions of great places to take children whilst visiting Auckland.

The **Sky Tower** in Auckland will certainly be the talk of any teen's experiences in New Zealand. Located 328 meters high, you travel upwards in glass elevators straight up to the viewing platform. Those who are over ten years old have the chance to do a Sky Walk or even a Sky Jump!

Sky Tower Website
https://www.skycityauckland.co.nz/attractions/sky-tower/
Sky Tower Map
https://goo.gl/maps/Pov6sad3C762
Phone : +64 9-363 6000
Address : Victoria St W & Federal St, Auckland 1010

Other places a bit closer to land include **Kelly Tarlton's Antarctic Encounter** and Underwater World; here visitors can enjoy learning more about a wide range of sea creatures and even allows you to get close to penguins and sharks!

Kelly Tarlton's Antarctic Encounter Website
https://www.kellytarltons.co.nz/
Kelly Tarlton's Antarctic Encounter Map
https://goo.gl/maps/CDufPgKEyWQ2
Phone : +64 9-531 5065
Address : 23 Tamaki Drive, Orakei, Auckland 1071

Head to the **Auckland Museum**, not only to see the interesting collections relating to New Zealand history but also for the amazing

Maori cultural shows, which are performed here on a daily basis. There are a variety of shows including a welcome dance, a weaponry display, and haka.

Auckland Museum Website
http://www.aucklandmuseum.com/
Auckland Museum Map
https://goo.gl/maps/U8mcfn6oEKu
Phone :+64 9-309 0443
Address : The Auckland Domain, Parnell, Auckland 1010

For children who enjoy more blood-rushing activities head to **EcoZip Adventures**. Kids of all ages (and adults, too) can enjoy the best of zip lines, guaranteed to make anyone's blood pump with adrenaline. When you need them to calm down a little, there are some impressive walks on Waiheke Island through an eco-immersive forest.

EcoZip Adventures Website
http://www.ecozipadventures.co.nz/
EcoZip Adventures Map
https://goo.gl/maps/NztMkjdWLKE2
Phone :+64 9-372 5646
Address : 150 Trig Hill Rd, Onetangi, Auckland 1081

For animal lovers, **Auckland Zoo** is a great place to visit. It houses more than 700 animals of 117 different species, and hosts a number of shows and events throughout the year. Visitors can even participate in events where you can get up close with a variety of different animals alongside zookeepers. Another great animal center to visit with kids is SheepWorld, which houses an array of farm animals.

Auckland Zoo Website
http://www.aucklandzoo.co.nz/default
Auckland Zoo Map
https://goo.gl/maps/LpYCoJ2dck62
Phone :+64 9-360 3805
Address :Motions Rd, Auckland 1022

If you need more exciting places, head to **Rainbows End Adventure Park**, located at Manukau City, which features some impressive rides for all ages.

Rainbows End Adventure Park Website
http://rainbowsend.co.nz/
Rainbows End Adventure Park Map
https://goo.gl/maps/yx1mZ1Xmgsj
Phone :+64 9-262 2030
Address :2 Clist Cres, Manukau, Auckland 2104

If you looking for a nice shopping area in Auckland, check out **Ponsonby**.Ponsonby is filled with up-market shops, cafes, art galleries, restaurants and night clubs.

Ponsonby Website
http://www.aucklandnz.com/discover/ponsonby
Ponsonby Map
https://goo.gl/maps/E7AijovMYyQ2

Hotels, Restaurants, and Bars
I have put together a list of the best Hotels, Restaurants, and Bars for you to visit in Auckland.

Hotels
Abaco On Jervois Website
http://www.abaco.co.nz/
Abaco On Jervois Map
https://goo.gl/maps/7Kzmm7ZEE1P2

Tel:+64 800 220 066
Address :57-59 Jervois Rd, Ponsonby,
Auckland 1011

Mollies Hotel Website
http://www.mollies.co.nz/
Mollies Hotel Map
https://goo.gl/maps/3KFk6rhwvVC2
Tel:+64 9-376 3489
Address :6 Tweed St, Auckland 1011

Verandahs Backpacker Lodge Website
http://www.verandahs.co.nz/home.html
Verandahs Backpacker Lodge Map
https://goo.gl/maps/PoEz7otokrA2
Tel:+64 9-360 4180
Address :6 Hopetoun St, Freemans Bay, Auckland 1011

Adina Apartment Hotel Website
https://www.tfehotels.com/brands/adina-
apartment-hotels/adina-apartment-hotel-
auckland-britomart
Adina Apartment Hotel Map
https://goo.gl/maps/CNevhbkLWw22
Tel:+64 9-393 8200
Address :2 Tapora St, Auckland, 1010

Stamford Plaza Website
http://www.stamford.com.au/spak
Stamford Plaza Map
https://goo.gl/maps/9uZJ69MdRTK2
Tel:+64 9-309 8888
Address :22-26 Albert St, Auckland, 1010

Bethells Beach Cottages Website
http://www.bethellsbeach.com/
Bethells Beach Cottages Map
https://goo.gl/maps/m2aoLKFx5BP2
Tel:+64 9-810 9581
Address :267 Bethells Rd, Bethells Beach 0781

Auckland North Shore Motels & Holiday Park Website
http://www.top1.co.nz/
Auckland North Shore Motels & Holiday Park Map
https://goo.gl/maps/EZcPhQE7JB72
Tel:+64 9-418 2578
Address :52 Northcote Rd, Northcote, Auckland 0627

Restaurants
Coco's Cantina Website
http://cocoscantina.co.nz/
Coco's Cantina Map
https://goo.gl/maps/zsS4amD7EWC2
Phone :+64 9-300 7582
Address :376 Karangahape Rd, 1010

Bellota Website
https://www.skycityauckland.co.nz/bars/bellota/
Bellota Map
https://goo.gl/maps/yhAZMDtkZwP2
Phone :+64 9-363 6000
Address :91 Federal St, Auckland, 1010

Prego Website
http://www.prego.co.nz/menus
Prego Map
https://goo.gl/maps/MV1VDbgZcNm

Phone :+64 9-376 3095
Address :226 Ponsonby Rd, 1011

SPQR Website
http://spqrnz.co.nz/
SPQR Map
https://goo.gl/maps/Gh4yF16w5No
Phone :+64 9-360 1710
Address :150 Ponsonby Rd, Ponsonby, Auckland 1011

Cafe Hanoi Website
http://www.cafehanoi.co.nz/
Cafe Hanoi Map
https://goo.gl/maps/tJUzKS4SBq72
Phone :+64 9-302 3478
Address :Excelsior Building Galway Street &
Commerce Street, Britomart, Auckland 1010

Molten Website
http://molten.co.nz/
Molten Map
https://goo.gl/maps/erKVybhWZtJ2
Phone :+64 9-638 7236
Address :422 Mount Eden Rd, Auckland 1024

Matakana Website
http://www.visitmatakana.co.nz/
Matakana Map
https://goo.gl/maps/YyM8CbQYv2r

Bars in Auckland

Kings Arms Tavern Website
http://www.kingsarms.co.nz/
Kings Arms Tavern Map
https://goo.gl/maps/hZD2p3ncS5k
Phone :+64 9-373 3240
Address :59 France St S, Eden Terrace, Auckland 1010

Tyler Street Garage Website
http://tylerstreetgarage.co.nz/
Tyler Street Garage Map
https://goo.gl/maps/xGpUfUdvY8Q2
Phone :+64 9-300 5279
Address :120 Quay St, Auckland, 1010

The Golden Dawn Website
http://www.goldendawn.co.nz/p/whats-on.html
The Golden Dawn Map
https://goo.gl/maps/mtEG43PyPBn
Phone :+64 9-376 9929
Address :134 Ponsonby Rd, Ponsonby,
Auckland 1011

16 Tun Website
http://16tun.co.nz/
16 Tun Map
https://goo.gl/maps/r1rPVrZYitw
Phone :+64 9-368 7712
Address :10/26 Jellicoe St, Auckland, 1050

Basque Kitchen Bar Website
https://www.facebook.com/pages/Basque-
Kitchen-and-Bar/198868770129155
Basque Kitchen Bar Map

https://goo.gl/maps/dNo45UDdkJR2
Phone :+64 9-523 1057
Address :61-73 Davis Cres, Newmarket,
Auckland 1023

Bedford Soda and Liquor Website
http://www.bedfordsodaliquor.co.nz/
Bedford Soda and Liquor Map
https://goo.gl/maps/7zTGFYAEmGT2
Phone :+64 9-378 7362
Address :4 Brown St, Ponsonby,
Auckland 1011

8

The Coromandel

Head to the **Coromandel** and immerse yourself in ancient forests, gorgeous coastline, soft sandy beaches and relax. This region is well known for its relaxing atmosphere, and with a number of great towns, cities, and attractions, it has become a popular region for international visitors.

The Coromandel Website
http://www.thecoromandel.com/
The Coromandel Map
https://goo.gl/maps/vqH8uJM2SQs

Thames and Thames Coast

Thames and the Thames Coast is an area of outstanding natural beauty, rich in history as well as being home to some natural wonders. The region is best known for its gold mining history. If you are interested in learning more about this subject then head to the **Thames School of Mines and Mineralogical Museum**; other great places to learn about local history are the Thames Historical Museum and the **Bella Street Pumphouse**.

Thames Coast Website
http://www.thamesinfo.co.nz/home
Thames Coast Map
https://goo.gl/maps/8y7CFr3onPy

Thames School of Mines and Mineralogical
 Museum Map
https://goo.gl/maps/3ThcyMgKD092
Thames Historical Museum Map
https://goo.gl/maps/nFKhHeiAr1S2
Phone :+64 7-868 8509
Address :Cochrane St, Waikato 3500

Bella Street Pumphouse Website
http://www.bellastreetpumphouse.com/

For nature lovers, there are an immense number of places you can try. Don't miss out on the chance to visit the **Butterfly and Orchid Garden**, Karaka Birdhide and the **Rapaura Water Gardens**. From the end of November, the beautiful Pohutukawa Tree bursts into scarlet flowers, making them a beautiful sight to behold. Over 100 different species of birds settle on the borders of the **Firth of Thames** and it's always fun to try to spot as many as you can as you drive your way through this area. After a hard day's exploring, pay a visit to the **Miranda Hot Springs** and relax in the soothing mineral waters, not far from the Miranda Shorebird Centre.

Butterfly and Orchid Garden Website
http://www.butterfly.co.nz/
Butterfly and Orchid Garden Map
https://goo.gl/maps/jwyTcfjcFir
Phone :+64 7-868 8080
Address :115 Victoria St, Thames 3500

Rapaura Water Gardens Website
http://www.rapaurawatergardens.co.nz/
Rapaura Water Gardens Map
https://goo.gl/maps/wapWjHFfomJ2
Phone :+64 7-868 4821
Address :586 Tapu Coroglen Rd, Thames 3575

Firth of Thames Map
https://goo.gl/maps/TGRwv4PLX892

Miranda Hot Springs Website
http://www.mirandahotsprings.co.nz/
Miranda Hot Springs Map
https://goo.gl/maps/3rsCBjZBTg12
Phone :+64 7-867 3055
Address :Front Miranda Rd, RD 6, Thames,
Miranda 3576

Miranda Shorebird Centre Website
http://www.miranda-shorebird.org.nz/
Miranda Shorebird Centre Map
https://goo.gl/maps/PYj64WpVP7P2
Phone :+64 9-232 2781
Address :283 E Coast Rd, Pokeno 2473

Adrenaline junkies of all ages will enjoy taking a trip to **Canyonz**. A trip here will offer you an extraordinary canyon experience that will stay with you for years to come. It is located just outside of Thames within the Kauaeranga Valley Sleeping God Canyon. When you've finished here and still in need of more blood-pumping activities, head to the **Hauraki Rail Trail** where you can go mountain bike riding and hiking. Other great places for these activities include

Rocky's Goldmine Walk and the **Thames coastal walkway**. For those interested in tramping then The Pinnacles, situated in the Kauaeranga Valley, is the ideal destination. The views over the mountainous ridges are breathtaking.

Canyonz Website
http://www.canyonz.co.nz/
Canyonz Map
https://goo.gl/maps/TvcQLqDvyG22
Phone :+64 21 456 682
Address :200 Mary St, Thames 3500

Hauraki Rail Trail Website
http://www.haurakirailtrail.co.nz/
Hauraki Rail Trail Map
https://goo.gl/maps/9t9Wj3ZMQi92
Phone :07 868 5140 (within NZ)
+64 7 868 5140 (international)
Address :407 Mackay Street, Thames, Coromandel
Hauraki, North Island

Rocky's Goldmine Walk Website
http://www.dicksonpark.co.nz/rockys.php
Rocky's Goldmine Walk Map
https://goo.gl/maps/v8HEMqTH27G2
Phone :+64 7-868 7308
Address :115 Victoria St, Thames 3500

The Pinnacles Website
http://www.thecoromandel.com/activities/
must-do/the-pinnacles/
The Pinnacles Map

https://goo.gl/maps/761oDorzPW92

9

Whitianga and Mercury Bay

The coastal town of **Whitianga** is the ideal place to stay if you want to explore Mercury Bay and the surrounding region. The area is well known for its stunning natural scenery and boasts a wonderful array of things to see and do, no matter how old you are.

Whitianga Website
http://www.whitianga.co.nz/

Whitianga Map
https://goo.gl/maps/yoWDvTfdLYR2

Mercury Bay Website
http://mercurybay.co.nz/
Mercury Bay Map
https://goo.gl/maps/1PHCXgT2aw32

Hot Water Beach is a popular place to visit, especially since you dig your own personal spa pool and relax in the warm waters – the perfect reward for all that hard work! Head to **Cathedral Cove**, known for its distinctive arch made from rock, for swimming, sunbathing, snorkeling and diving opportunities.

Hot Water Beach Website
http://www.whitianga.co.nz/about/discover-hotwater-beach
Hot Water Beach Map
https://goo.gl/maps/TGEwTjHtqm12

Cathedral Cove Website
http://www.thecoromandel.com/activities/must-do/cathedral-cove/
Cathedral Cove Map
https://goo.gl/maps/fRyiyD2bejx

There are a number of other things to do here. Why not spend some time getting to know the local arts' scene? There are several great **art galleries** and studios that are open to the public as well as various restaurants offering delicious dishes of all kinds. After you've had your fill of food and art, why not visit The Lost Spring, one of the more recent thermal hot pools to open in the country.

Art Website
http://www.mercurybayartescape.com/Mosaic.html
Phone :07 866 5224
Address :53 Albert St,Whitianga

The landscape of Whitianga and Mercury Bay is often referred to as though it was plucked out of an artist's imagination and made real. The coastline is volcanic and dotted with picturesque sea caves. There are several boat companies offering tours and if you wish you can explore them yourself by hiring a kayak and paddling along the coastline. Otherwise, you can jump on a ferry and visit a number of places worth seeing including **Shakespeare's Cliff**. Top beaches in the area include **Opito and Kuaotunu.**

Shakespeare's Cliff Website
http://www.hahei.co.nz/cooks-beach.html
Shakespeare's Cliff Map
https://goo.gl/maps/DaF9qRZ4zpN2

Opito Beach Map
https://goo.gl/maps/qdQSdc2Kg8U2

Kuaotunu Beach Website
http://www.whitianga.co.nz/about/discover-kuaotunu
Kuaotunu Beach Map
https://goo.gl/maps/FjGEaRWTcH82

Paeroa
Located between Auckland and Tauranga, **Paeroa** is a beautiful place to stop and explore. This is the place where the famous Lemon and Paeroa drink was created – a beverage that must be sampled if you

visit here. The restaurants in Paeroa cater to all tastes and budgets, and there are several good attractions well worth visiting.

Paeroa Map
https://goo.gl/maps/x4bcqbhVBgP2

Lemon and Paeroa Drink Website
http://www.lpcafe.co.nz/
Lemon and Paeroa Drink Map
https://goo.gl/maps/USqLSdKxRoG2
Phone :+64 7-862 6753
Address :2 Seymour St, Paeroa 3600

The town is well known for its antique shops (but make sure you are allowed to take anything you buy out of the country before you part ways with your money). You can even start on the **Hauraki Rail Trail** from Paeroa. The water gardens are a great place to visit, ideal if you want somewhere relaxing to enjoy.

Hauraki Rail Trail Website
http://www.haurakirailtrail.co.nz/
Hauraki Rail Trail Map
https://goo.gl/maps/tkrUgafUPa22
Phone :07 868 5140 (within NZ)
+64 7 868 5140 (international)
Address :407 MacKay Street, Thames 3500

Eastland
Eastland is famous for being the point where the first Polynesians arrived so many centuries ago, as well as being the location where Captain Cook first arrived and where the Maori and the Europeans first made contact with each other. As a result, the area is steeped in history as well as boasting a beautiful landscape which is actually less

explored compared to other regions in New Zealand.

Eastland Website
http://www.outeast.co.nz/
Eastland Map
https://goo.gl/maps/dNk1WvnczZp

Maori Culture

While visitors to New Zealand can get to know the Maori and learn more about their rich history and culture, Eastland is one of the best destinations to visit for this. There are numerous Maori-related trips you can participate in. For example, join a tour group (via a four by four or a hiking trip) which takes you up **Mount Hikurangi** to view the Maori engravings and learn how the demi-god Maui fished North Island up from beneath the waves.

Mount Hikurangi Website
http://www.doc.govt.nz/parks-and-recreation/places-to
-go/east-coast/places/raukumara-conservation-park
/things-to-do/mount-hikurangi-te-ara-ki-hikurangi/
Mount Hikurangi Map
https://goo.gl/maps/AunC2EtqNC12

If you wish to visit **Te Poho O Rawiri Marae** then you will need to book in advance, but it is well worth it. The whare rununga, the traditional Maori meeting house, is inundated with exceptionally beautiful carvings and woven panels called tukutuku. The Maori church known as Tikitiki Church is an outstandingly beautiful religious building featuring richly elaborate stained glass windows. For those wanting to learn more about the Maori, why not join a Maori cultural trip to learn about the history and traditions of the Maori from the Eastland region.

Te Poho O Rawiri Marae Website
http://www.ngatiporou.com/nati-life/ngati-porou
-marae/te-poho-o-rawiri-marae
Te Poho O Rawiri Marae Map
https://goo.gl/maps/hJ7PZkjFRB42
Phone: +64 6 864 9004

It's Time for an Adventure!

If you are searching for an exciting time in New Zealand then the Eastland region will certainly not let you down. The natural landscape has provided visitors with a variety of things to see and do. For those whose hearts' can take it, why not try **diving with sharks** (in a cage, obviously) or feed stingrays? For slightly less heart-pumping action, there are tour guides offering rafting trips down the **Motu River**, the thrilling Rere Rock Slide is a naturally occurring rock sliding experience, or why not go **mountain biking** on the Motu Trails or **hike** the Te Urewera, the biggest forest on the North Island. For those wanting a relaxing time, then ocean fishing trips are aplenty in Eastland.

Cage Diving Website
http://divenewzealand.co.nz/article-564/

Motu River Jet Boat Website
http://www.moturiverjet.com/
Phone: +64 (07) 315 5028
Address: Opotiki i-Site ,70 Bridge Street

Rere Rock Slide Map
https://goo.gl/maps/nBXQL4CbVxG2
Address: Wharekopae Rd, Ngatapa 4072

Motu River New Zealand Map
https://goo.gl/maps/nTm1f9dXqs12

Te Urewera Hikes Website
http://www.teureweratreks.co.nz/
Te Urewera Hikes Map
https://goo.gl/maps/8j8jRwNkFFp
Phone: +64 7-929 9669
Address: 3891 Ruatahuna Rd, Bay of Plenty,
Ruatahuna 3079

Experience the Beauty of the Region

New Zealand is world famous for its beautiful scenery and Eastland is certainly no exception. You can enjoy this beauty in a number of ways. Why not visit **Rere Falls**, a majestic waterfall which you can explore behind; take in the outstanding vistas over Poverty Bay from **Kaiti Hill**; soak in the relaxing waters of Nikau Pools at the Morere Hot Springs, surrounded by forests; **Lake Waikaremoana** offers fishing, swimming, and other activities for all ages; the Waioeka Scenic Reserve is ideal for those wanting to explore the bush; and certainly visit **Gisborne**, the area referred to as the Chardonnay Capital of New Zealand, boasting excellent wineries which offer tours and sampling opportunities.

Rere Falls Website
http://waterfalls.co.nz/waterfalls-by-region
/83-new-zealand-waterfalls/north-island/hawkesbay
/209-rere-falls
Rere Falls Map
https://goo.gl/maps/G5G2276W5EM2
Address: Wharekopae River, Gisborne, Rere 4072

Kaiti Hill Map
https://goo.gl/maps/zesaQLDkNnw

Morere Hot Springs Website
http://morerehotsprings.co.nz/
Morere Hot Springs Map
https://goo.gl/maps/uahqHyteCMo
Phone: +64 6-837 8856

Address: SH 2, Nuhaka 4078

Lake Waikaremoana Website
http://www.walkinglegends.com/new-zealand-guided
-walks-snapshot/lake-waikaremoana
-guided-walk/
Lake Waikaremoana Map
https://goo.gl/maps/JfxKFs2yeKs

Waioeka Scenic Reserve Website
http://www.doc.govt.nz/parks-and-recreation/
places-to-go/east-coast/places/waioeka
-gorge-scenic-reserve/

Gisborne Website
http://www.cityofgisborne.co.nz/
Gisborne Map
https://goo.gl/maps/PVsh5PzW2MT2

10

Taranaki

Many visitors head to **Taranaki** solely for the purpose of climbing up the mountain, but there are a number of towns, cities, national parks and other attractions well worth seeing.

Taranaki Website
http://www.visit.taranaki.info/
Taranaki Map
https://goo.gl/maps/5GHCzPw5WXz

Egmont National Park
Mount Taranaki is located within the **Egmont National Park**. As previously mentioned, visitors head straight for it but the park offers a wonderful menu of things to do here. Start with hiking up to the

mountain peak or hike along the Pouakai Crossing trail but anyone attempting the latter in winter will need to have experience hiking across snow and ice.

Numerous walking trails around the mountain offer visitors the chance to see some beautiful sights, with the smallest lasting 10 minutes and the largest trails taking up to three days. For those of you wanting to experience the magic of the mountain but not wanting to get sweaty or exhausted seeing it, take to the skies! There are **helicopter tours** of Mount Taranaki on offer. Last but certainly not least, the Stratford Mountain Club offers skiing at Manganui between June and October.

Egmont National Park Website
http://www.doc.govt.nz/parks-and-recreation
/places-to-go/taranaki/places
/egmont-national-park/
Egmont National Park Hiking Website
http://www.backpackerguide.nz/6-hikes-egmont-national-park/

Egmont National Park Map
https://goo.gl/maps/sFX6krzxWFM2
Phone: +64 6-756 0990

Helicopter Tours Website
http://www.heli.co.nz/scenic-flights-2/
Phone: 0800 33 66 44
Address: 4512 Mountain Road (SHY 3) Eltham ,4322

Surfing and the Coastline

Due to its dramatic coastline that curls around on a north to west positioning, there are ample opportunities to go surfing in Taranaki – indeed, this region claims to be the best when it comes to surfing.

For those of you that enjoy surfing head to **Surf Highway 45,** which will take you to all the best surfing spots in the region. At Sugarloaf Marine Park you can come up close with seals and other sea-dwelling creatures. If you don't have any or much experience, then there are

surfing schools where you can take lessons.

Surf Highway 45 Map
https://goo.gl/maps/kxYtMoPAoF62

Sugarloaf Marine Park Website
http://www.doc.govt.nz/parks-and-
recreation/places-to-go/taranaki/places
/nga-motu-sugar-loaf-islands/
Sugarloaf Marine Park Map
https://goo.gl/maps/AuWDdiYDTvE2

Surf School Website
https://taranakisurfschool.com/
Phone : 021-119-6218

For those who enjoy the coast but don't fancy getting wet, there are a number of attractions to see. The **Cape Egmont Lighthouse**, with Mount Taranaki behind it, offers a beautiful backdrop for photo shoots. Then head onto the famous **Whitecliffs Walkway**, this five-hour walkway takes you to the renowned white cliffs, the **Three Sisters** rocks and then the man-made Te Horo tunnel. If this wasn't enough walking for you, then you could hike up the volcanic Paritutu Roc, which rewards you with outstanding views of the dramatic coastline.

Cape Egmont Lighthouse Map
https://goo.gl/maps/91fAvc7ELov

Whitecliffs Walkway Website
http://www.doc.govt.nz/parks-and-recreation
/places-to-go/taranaki/places/white-cliffs
-and-mount-messenger-conservation-area
/things-to-do/whitecliffs-walkway/

The Best of Art, History and Culture

Taranaki offers an **amazing array of art**, cultural and historical activities and sites to visit, all designed to open the mind and allow beauty to inspire you. Read on to discover some of the best artistic, cultural and historical attractions in Taranaki.

Located in New Plymouth's waterfront, **Puke Ariki** is a fantastic **museum** dedicated to illustrating the history of this region. There are historical tours available which allow history – particularly the **Taranaki Land Wars** in the 19th century – to come to life. You could also stroll along the 11-kilometer walkway, a path offering dramatic vistas over the coastline, rock pools, and the stunning **Te Rewa Rewa Bridge**.

Puke Ariki Website
http://pukeariki.com/
Puke Ariki Map
https://goo.gl/maps/foZCg1UGwd52
Phone : +64 6-759 6060
Address :1 Ariki St, New Plymouth 4310

Taranaki Land Wars Website
http://pukeariki.com/Exhibitions/Exhibitions
-Archive/Taranaki-War

Te Rewa Rewa Bridge Map
https://goo.gl/maps/n3fjTcbzNfN2

For art lovers, the **Govett-Brewster Art Gallery** and the Len Lye Centre are the ideal attractions to visit, while culture buffs will enjoy learning about the early history of the Maori and European settlers at the fabulous **Tawhiti Museum**. For the younger audience, or just the young at heart, the **Fun Ho National Toy Museum**, showcasing more than 3000 toys created locally since the 1930s.

Govett-Brewster Art Galler Website
http://www.govettbrewster.com/
Govett-Brewster Art Galler Map
https://goo.gl/maps/upsBVheeEUP2
Phone : +64 6-759 6060
Address :42 Queen St, New Plymouth 4310

Tawhiti Museum Website
http://www.tawhitimuseum.co.nz/
Tawhiti Museum Map
https://goo.gl/maps/3xwQq6ZJz6m
Phone : +64 6-278 6837
Address : 401 Ohangai Rd, Hawera 4672,

Fun Ho National Toy Museum Website
http://www.funhotoys.co.nz/
Fun Ho National Toy Museum Map
https://goo.gl/maps/KwMgsYU9Nfm
Phone : +64 6-756 7030
Address : 25 Rata St, Inglewood 4330

Other top attractions in the region include **Pioneer Village in Strat-ford**, the **Forgotten World Highway** and a number of elite wineries offering sampling tours.

Pioneer Village Website
http://www.pioneervillage.co.nz/
Pioneer Village Map
https://goo.gl/maps/upJ7rHtVAx52
Phone : +64 6-765 5399
Address : 3912 Mountain Rd, Stratford 4393

Forgotten World Highway Map
https://goo.gl/maps/hz4AiuNhqux

11

Ruapehu

Whether you are looking for a dose of history and culture or immerse yourself in adrenaline-pumping activities, you will find everything you need within the **Ruapehu** region.

Ruapehu Website
http://www.visitruapehu.com/
Ruapehu Map

https://goo.gl/maps/DcWbFDzk8tC2

Exploring Volcanoes and Rugged Landscapes

The region of Ruapehu is well known for its highly dramatic and rugged landscape. Not only is it beautiful, but it also provides a number of thrilling activities and sights to behold.

The **Tongariro Alpine Crossing** may only take a day to complete but it is one of the best walks in the country and certainly not for the faint-hearted. The 17-kilometer hike takes you past Mount Ngauruhoe and then across Mount Tongariro itself. Along the way you will see active volcanic locations, crater lakes that are almost too beautiful for words and vistas that look as though they were plucked from an artist's imagination. Another great circuit to try is the Tongariro Northern Circuit, one of the top nine walks in the country; this three or four-day hike is 41 kilometers long, with the first day following the previously mentioned Tongariro Alpine Crossing.

Ruapehu Ski and Snowboard Website
http://www.mtruapehu.com/
Phone : +64 6 385 8456

Tongariro Alpine Crossing Website
http://www.tongarirocrossing.org.nz/
Tongariro Alpine Crossing Map
https://goo.gl/maps/4QDgmwDAdY22

Tongariro Northern Circuit Map
https://goo.gl/maps/B1HTPLLGquP2

For visitors who love to ski then definitely pay a visit to **Whakapapa**. Located on Mount Ruapehu, this is the most popular **ski field** in the country, boasting 500 hectares of skiing territory and 400 hectares accessible by lifts. Another popular ski resort in this region is the Turoa

Ski Field, located on the southern slopes of Mount Ruapehu. Known by locals and visitors alike as The Giant, Turoa Ski Field boasts 500 hectares of ski slopes and 400 hectares of beautiful land that you can explore on horseback or quad bikes.

Whakapapa Map
https://goo.gl/maps/Rzrkcyy6CHw

Turoa Ski Field Map
https://goo.gl/maps/tqPH9abL5k22
Phone : +64 6-385 8456

If skiing isn't your thing then you can try **mountain biking**. The 42 Traverse is a well-known trail heading down 570 meters through the Tongariro Forest Park. There are a number of old logger's tracks in the Rangataua Forest that provide some amazing mountain bike trails to follow and if this wasn't enough, then the Ohakune Mountain Road is perfect for biking during the summer since the trail leads downhill!

Mountain Biking Website
http://www.tongarironationalpark.com/
activities/tongariro-mountain-biking.html
Phone : 64-7-892 2991

Relaxing in Style
Within the Ruapehu region, there are numerous luxury resorts and attractions that are all designed to make you feel relaxed and experience the beauty of the area in style. **Chateau Tongariro** and the **Grand Chateau** are the perfect base for those visiting the local skiing facilities but want style and comfort.

Chateau Tongariro Hotel Website
http://www.chateau.co.nz/
Chateau Tongariro Hotel Map
https://goo.gl/maps/keSNocCkHGF2
Tel:+64 7-892 3809

To see the region in style why not take a private helicopter or plane ride over the mountains to see the region the way most visitors never get the chance to. The Whakapapa River provides the best trout fishing, or you can simply relax in the **hot springs at Tokaanu** – the opportunities are limitless.

Tokaanu Hot Springs Website
http://www.nzhotpools.co.nz/hot-pools/tokaanu-thermal-pools/
Tokaanu Hot Springs Map
https://goo.gl/maps/4bzf2DRkzUT2

Phone : +64 7-386 8575
Address : Mangaroa St, Tokaanu 3381

History
For history lovers make time to explore some of the region's museums. The **Queen Elizabeth II Army Memorial Museum** located in Waiouru contains some amazing artifacts relating to the New Zealand Land Wars and from the other wars the country experience during the 20th century.

The Queen Elizabeth II Army Memorial Museum Website
http://www.armymuseum.co.nz/
The Queen Elizabeth II Army Memorial Museum Map
https://goo.gl/maps/ys5TezyeBL52
Phone : +64 6-387 6911
Address : State Highway One & Hassett Drive, Waiouru 4861

Another delight is the **Raurimu Spiral**, a feat of fantastic engineering on the North Island Main Trunk Railway – it is so popular that train lovers come here from all corners of the world to visit it.

Raurimu Spiral Map
https://goo.gl/maps/eqMPC5CXp8J2

Lake Taupo
Another popular attraction in Ruapehu is Lake Taupo. Here you can get back to nature, allow your soul to take flight with the beauty of the area and take in a range of activities in and around the lake. Lake Taupo boasts a number of beaches and caves, perfect for exploring via kayak. Don't miss out on seeing the Maori Rock Carvings located at **Mine Bay** – the only way to see them is via water.

Lake Taupo Website
http://www.greatlaketaupo.com/
Lake Taupo Map
https://goo.gl/maps/7eitWRSMMb62
Phone: +64 7 376 0027

Mine Bay Map
https://goo.gl/maps/sSvev10osVQ2

Lake Taupo is popular with those who like to fish. The lake is home to rainbow and brown trout, and there are local guides who will take you fly-fishing on Tongariro River.

Around Lake Taupo, visitors can visit the geothermal mud pools – still active today – and the steam vents at Caters of the Moon and at Orakei Korako. For hikers, the scenery through the Whirinaki rainforests and **Pureora Forest Park** is exceptional.

Pureora Forest Park Map
https://goo.gl/maps/CysvhWRzF9E2

Relaxation

Relaxation can be enjoyed indoors or outdoors in Ruapehu. Why not enjoy a calming picnic beside Lake Taupo or take a refreshing dip in the crystal clear waters? There are a number of hot spring resorts within the area – the geothermal waters well known for releasing tension in the body.

If this wasn't enough, Ruapehu boasts six golf clubs and dozens of stylish restaurants. Definitely pay a visit to **Huka Prawn Park** where the seafood is famous.

Huka Prawn Park Website
http://www.hukaprawnpark.co.nz/
Huka Prawn Park Map
https://goo.gl/maps/TyFjt3zGbsC2
Phone : (07) 374 8474

12

Hawke's Bay

Hawke's Bay is often referred to as New Zealand's Wine Country, but scratch beneath the surface and you will discover there is so much more to this region than just wine – although the wine should certainly be sampled.

Hawke's Bay Website
http://www.hawkesbaynz.com/

Hawke's Bay Map
https://goo.gl/maps/2seHb2D6JYG2

This is also one of the driest areas within the country, which makes it perfect for growing grapes, particularly Cabernet Sauvignon and Syrah. Hawke's Bay is the beginning of the **Classic New Zealand Wine Trail** and there are many wine tours that are popular.

Classic New Zealand Wine Trail Website
http://www.wellingtonnz.com/classic-
new-zealand-wine-trail/

In addition to being the best place for wine in New Zealand, Hawke's Bay is also known for being the Art Deco Center of the country. A massive earthquake devastated the region in the 1930s and so was rebuilt in this iconic style. It is also home to the best Matariki celebrations, the Maori New Year. Hawke's Bay is the ideal base for parties who enjoy a range of activities since you can visit Napier's Great Long Lunch, explore the trails at **Kaweka Forest Park**, see the beauty of the sandy beaches and then explore Cape Kidnappers Gannet Colony.

Kaweka Forest Park Map
https://goo.gl/maps/FjG1cxFettF2

13

Manawatu

Manawatu is a region located in the lower heartland of North Island. Visiting here offers guests a chance to see a different part of New Zealand's unique character and certainly not a region to miss on seeing.

This region is home to the **Ruahine Forest Park**, an area of exceptional beauty offering tramping tracks and a range of accommodation. The trails here are mostly uphill and can be taxing for those who don't have much experience but the vistas at the top, stretching from the forests to the oceans, are well worth the effort.

Manawatu Website
http://www.manawatunz.co.nz/
Manawatu Map
https://goo.gl/maps/G63KP9CQaj62

Ruahine Forest Park Website
http://www.doc.govt.nz/parks-and-recreation/
places-to-go/manawatu-whanganui/places
/ruahine-forest-park/
Ruahine Forest Park Map
https://goo.gl/maps/Awx3fg7vncE2

As you explore this region you will most likely come across many beautiful colorful gardens – Manawatu is abound with gardeners who take their gardens very seriously. Some of the best to see here are the **Palmerston North's Victoria Esplanade Gardens** and **Kimbolton's Cross Hills Garden**.

Palmerston North's Victoria Esplanade Gardens Map
https://goo.gl/maps/EEZX24Hp9DF2

Kimbolton's Cross Hills Garden Map
https://goo.gl/maps/baQ43UjJNo52

The Country Road
The Country Road takes you away from the highway and allows you to explore various landscapes as you make your way through Manawatu. There are a number of towns and scenic points to stop off at along various routes:

The **Stormy Point Route** is located within Taupo and Wellington, inundated with beautiful scenery, including scenic points over the river.

Try to take the Peep-O-Day Route, named for the Peep-O-Day Scenic Point, where the sun first rises in the morning.

Stormy Point Route Website
http://www.manawatunz.co.nz/visit/see-do /scenic-journeys/
The Stormy Point Route Map
https://goo.gl/maps/MaSJtF2NnuE2

The **Pohangina Valley Route** is popular with tourists who want to see the 'back country' of the region. It takes you through the Pohangina Valley, which begins at the base of the Ruahine Mountain Range, where a number of quiet villages are based in addition to the Totara Reserve Regional Park.

Pohangina Valley Website
http://www.pohanginavalleyestate.co.nz/
Pohangina Valley Map
https://goo.gl/maps/ZXrVW3RBw822

The **Iron Gates Experience** is located in the northern part of Man-awatu where visitors can engage in a number of activities including horse riding, hiking, camping and boasts various natural sites to see.

The Iron Gates Experience Website
http://www.irongates.co.nz/
The Iron Gates Experience Map
https://goo.gl/maps/mmFG3x9yjX92
Phone : +64 6-328 2841
Address : 981 Main South Rd, 4774

Whanganui

Translating as 'Big Bay' or 'Big Harbor', Whanganui is one of the oldest cities in the country and is named after the river, which snakes its way through the city.

Whanganui Website
http://whanganuinz.com/
Wanganui Map
https://goo.gl/maps/BdWdLj6TDTS2

Also spelled Wanganui, the city is home to around 43,000 people and still retains much of its original settler vibe even though it is still a thoroughly modern city. This contradiction makes Whanganui a unique place to visit; popular with international tourists as it is only located a few hours' drive from Wellington or even a short flight from Auckland.

Whanganui is a great place to explore even if you only have a day or two to do it in. The city boasts a flourishing arts' scene, claiming that more artists live here than anywhere else in the city. The **Whanganui Opera House**, the Glass School, and the Sarjeant Art Gallery are the best examples of the city's arts and culture scene to explore.

The Whanganui Opera House Website
http://www.royaloperahouse.co.nz/
The Whanganui Opera House Map
https://goo.gl/maps/yferu1yARTQ2
Phone :+64 6-349 0511
Address :69 St Hill St, Whanganui 4501

The **Whanganui River** has had a deep impact on the history and culture of the city since its early days. Snaking 260 kilometers towards the ocean, the river was used to help bring goods and Europeans to settle in the region, but it has also been a vital part of the Maori culture long before that. As a result, there are a number of attractions in and on the river that should not be missed out on.

Whanganui River Website
http://www.whanganuiriver.co.nz/
Whanganui River Map
https://goo.gl/maps/VWMkJcTrYTn

To learn more about the Maori of the area and how the river features in their culture, there are a number of river tours you can enjoy, including staying overnight at a traditional river Maori town. The **Whanganui Riverboat Centre** is a fantastic museum dedicated to the history of the river and oceans where visitors can enjoy the range of artifacts on display and cruises the center offers. As you go down the river, you will learn about the ancient Maori who lived along the river, the history of the European settlers and how the little towns along the way got their names.

The Whanganui Riverboat Centre Website
http://waimarie.co.nz/
The Whanganui Riverboat Centre Map
https://goo.gl/maps/vMtiwJyx5fo
Phone :+64 6-347 1863
Address :1A Taupo Quay, Whanganui 4500,

Accommodation and Restaurants: One of the best hotels in Whanganui is the **151 on London** with the best restaurants being the Springvale Café.

151 on London Hotel Website
http://www.151onlondon.co.nz/contact_us.htm

151 on London Hotel Map
https://goo.gl/maps/Ro9E2rruCfx
Phone:+64 6-345 8668
Address :151 London St, College Estate, Whanganui 4500

Springvale Cafe Website
http://www.springvalegardencentre.co.nz/main.html
Springvale Cafe Map
https://goo.gl/maps/Aj7NuSm4J6N2
Phone : +64 6-344 5846
Address : 18 Devon Road, Springvale, Whanganui 4501

14

Wellington

Wellington is the capital of New Zealand, located in the south of the North Island and boasts the charm of a small town but is big on style and pizzazz.

Wellington Website
http://www.wellingtonnz.com/
Wellington Map

https://goo.gl/maps/b6Ltg3KyitE2

Hollywood movie director Peter Jackson was born and raised in Wellington and has used the city as the backdrop for many movies, including The Hobbit: An Unexpected Journey in 2012. There are a number of walking tours that take you around some of the best sites in the city.

Wellington is said to boast more restaurants, bars and clubs per capita than New York; there are numerous restaurants catering to a wide range of cuisines, including numerous fine dining establishments around **Cuba Street.**

Cuba Street Map
https://goo.gl/maps/343LYwfKJdq
Cuba Street Website
http://www.wellingtonnz.com/media/
media-backgrounders/new-zealands-coolest-street/

Top Sights in Wellington
Wellington has a number of museums that offer intriguing glimpses into the history and culture of the country. **Te Papa** is one of the best museums in the world, offering state of the art exhibitions that showcase the history and art of New Zealand's people. Located on the waterfront, the museum is free for many exhibitions.

Te Papa Website
https://www.tepapa.govt.nz/
Te Papa Map
https://goo.gl/maps/YXbE4yK4X362
Phone :+64 4-381 7000
Address : 55 Cable St, Wellington 6011

For those traveling with children, pay a visit to the **Museum of Wellington City and Sea**. Another free museum, children will certainly enjoy the 'A Millennium Age', where Maori mythology is retold in a highly engaging manner. The Wahine shipwreck exhibition is another popular feature of the museum.

Museum of Wellington City and Sea Website
http://www.museumswellington.org.nz/
Museum of Wellington City and Sea Map
https://goo.gl/maps/ymUyz4Nzh2m
Phone :+64 4-472 8904
Address : Jervois Quay, Wellington 6011

At **Carter Observatory**, situated in the Botanical Gardens, you will find a mixture of science and Maori mythology. Come on Tuesdays and Saturdays where telescope viewings are permitted.

Wellington's art scene is highly praised; with several theaters and performance centers, there are numerous shows you can take in every single day of the week.

Carter Observatory Website
http://www.museumswellington.org.nz/space-place/
Carter Observatory Map
https://goo.gl/maps/zpwaswyYzWv
Phone :+64 4-910 3140
Address : 40 Salamanca Rd, Kelburn, Wellington 6012

Culture

When you visit Wellington, you will discover the history and legacy of the city. There are a number of attractions where you can discover this legacy in more detail.

Start with a renovated **cable car** trip from downtown Wellington. It takes you up to the Botanical Gardens and offers outstanding vistas over the capital and the harbor. To understand the political history of the country, why not take a guided tour of the Parliament Buildings or the Government Buildings that are situated opposite from each other.

One of the most renowned authors in New Zealand is Katherine Mansfield. She was born here in Wellington and visitors can take a tour of her home, which has undergone loving restorations so that it matches what her stories told.

Wellington Cable Car Website
http://www.wellingtoncablecar.co.nz/English/Home.html
Wellington Cable Car Map
https://goo.gl/maps/do3Cduqq1vS2
Phone :+64 4-472 2199
Address : 280 Lambton Quay, Wellington, 6011

Two more historical gems in Wellington are **St Paul's Cathedral**, with its beautiful Gothic façade, and the **Petone district**, inundated with art galleries, boutique stores, and stylish cafes.

St Paul's Cathedral Website
https://wellingtoncathedral.org.nz/
St Paul's Cathedral Map
https://goo.gl/maps/zww4gEgHesS2
Phone :+64 4-472 0286

Address : 45 Molesworth St, Thorndon, Wellington 6011

Petone District Website
http://www.jacksonstreet.co.nz/
Petone District Map
https://goo.gl/maps/SbQXAokRqC82

Natural Wellington
To really understand the beauty and culture of the city, Wellington boasts a number of attractions that highlight this aspect. Read on to find out more about these attractions.

Zealandia: the Karori Sanctuary Experience is located ten minutes away from the center of the city. This area is home to a number of rare animals that include the kiwi and tuatara and boasts a state of the art exhibition, which sets out its five hundred years conservation goal.

Wellington Zoo is not just the oldest zoo in the country – it is also one of the best attractions you can take your children to. Home to various species, it is a fantastic day out. More animal-based attractions include four by four guided trips to the nearby coastline where you can view colonies of New Zealand fur seals.

Zealandia Website
http://www.visitzealandia.com/plan-your-visit/
Zealandia Map
https://goo.gl/maps/SMWseYo9ZPT2
Phone :+64 4-920 9200
Address : 53 Waiapu Rd, Karori, Wellington 6012

There are numerous companies offering harbor cruises; one of the best trips is so **Somes Island**, also known as Matiu, which is located between Wellington Harbor and Days Bay. Wander around the little craft stores and cafes and immerse in the relaxing atmosphere.

Somes Island Ferry Website
http://eastbywest.co.nz/places-to-see/
Somes Island Map
https://goo.gl/maps/Q5Kdmatwuwx

For those who want to see more of the forested areas why not go mountain biking through **Makara Peak,** the rejuvenating bush which boasts a state of the art bike park.

Makara Peak Website
http://www.makarapeak.org/
Makara Peak Map
https://goo.gl/maps/Qgh8eAg9QW92
Address : 122 S Karori Rd, Wellington 6012

Within **Otari-Wilson Bush,** visitors will be amazed at the variety of flora, which grows in the country's sole botanical gardens devoted to the bush.

Otari-Wilson Bush Website
http://wellington.govt.nz/recreation
/enjoy-the-outdoors/gardens/otariwiltons
-bush/visitor-information
Otari-Wilson Bush Map
https://goo.gl/maps/jv8RCmY5F332
Phone :+64 4-499 1400
Address : 160 Wilton Rd, Wilton, Wellington 6012

Beaches and Scuba

Wellington has some beautiful beaches and is the scuba capital of New Zealand.Check out some of these beaches if you have time.

Scorching Bay Map
https://goo.gl/maps/KvZS39Hb6rz

Island Bay Map
https://goo.gl/maps/pQq1q48gwf62

Lyall Bay Map
https://goo.gl/maps/hSPZAxVuDxq

Oriental Bay Map
https://goo.gl/maps/pmp5jSweavs

Wellington Scuba Website
http://www.divewellington.co.nz/
Wellington Scuba Map
https://goo.gl/maps/dSaajFFyuu72
Phone :+64 4-939 3483

Address : 432 The Esplanade, Island Bay, Wellington 6023

Hotels, Restaurants, and Bars
I have put together a list of the best Hotels, Cafe's Restaurants, and Bars for you to visit in Wellington.

Hotels
Museum Art Hotel Wellington
http://www.museumhotel.co.nz/
Museum Art Hotel Wellington
https://goo.gl/maps/s57cpvvenz62
Tel:+64 4-802 8900
Address : 90 Cable St, Te Aro, Wellington 6011

Ohtel Website
https://www.ohtel.com/
Ohtel Map
https://goo.gl/maps/wM9NDX5DqD82
Tel:+64 4-803 0600
Address : 66 Oriental Parade, Oriental Bay, Wellington 6011

The Cambridge Hotel Website
http://cambridgehotel.co.nz/
The Cambridge Hotel Map
https://goo.gl/maps/QJLEDDQ46uE2
Tel:+64 4-385 8829
Address : 28 Cambridge Terrace, Te Aro, Wellington 6011

CQ Hotels Wellington Website
http://www.hotelwellington.co.nz/
CQ Hotels Wellington Map

https://goo.gl/maps/5kPDCZTDA5z
Tel:+64 4-385 2156
Address : 223 Cuba St, Te Aro, Wellington 6011

Hotel Waterloo & Backpackers Website
http://hotelwaterloo.co.nz/
Hotel Waterloo & Backpackers Map
https://goo.gl/maps/CUmsWe3cHz72
Tel:+64 4-473 84 82
Address :1 Bunny St, Pipitea, Wellington 6011

Coffee Shops
Customs by Coffee Supreme Website
http://www.coffeesupreme.com/
Customs by Coffee Supreme Map
https://goo.gl/maps/FEEQ8VQNHkz
Phone :+64 4-385 2129
Address :39 Ghuznee St, Te Aro, Wellington 6011

Baobab Cafe Website
http://baobabcafe.co.nz/about-us/
Baobab Cafe Map
https://goo.gl/maps/yWDf6SkhZ2L2
Phone :+64 4-380 0470
Address :152 Riddiford St, Newtown, Wellington 6021

Maranui Cafe Website
http://www.maranuicafe.co.nz/
Maranui Cafe Map
https://goo.gl/maps/tGs9x3GJ5FD2
Phone :+64 4-387 4539
Address :7 Lyall Parade, Lyall Bay, Wellington 6022

The Flight Coffee Hangar Website
http://flightcoffee.co.nz/pages/about-us
The Flight Coffee Hangar Map
https://goo.gl/maps/8BNK6ADwJv72
Phone :+64 4-830 0909
Address :119 Dixon St, Te Aro, Wellington 6011

Fidel's Cafe Website
http://www.fidelscafe.com/
Fidel's Cafe Map
https://goo.gl/maps/qvEQVJqve5k
Phone :+64 4-801 6868
Address :234 Cuba St, Wellington 6011

Restaurants
Ortega Website
http://ortega.co.nz/
Ortega Map
https://goo.gl/maps/DJy4fPw5po42
Phone :+64 4-382 9559
Address :16 Majoribanks St, Wellington 6011

Ancestral Website
http://www.ancestral.co.nz/
Ancestral Map
https://goo.gl/maps/ztsgJiapaE22
Phone :+64 4-801 8867
Address :31-33 Courtenay Pl, Te Aro, Wellington 6143

Charlie Bill - Fine Food Bistro Website
https://www.facebook.com/charliebillnz/
Charlie Bill - Fine Food Bistro Map
https://goo.gl/maps/kGE4JWrSKsp

Phone :+64 4-499 8464
Address :241 Tinakori Rd, Thorndon, Wellington 6011

Logan Brown Map
https://www.loganbrown.co.nz/
Logan Brown Website
https://goo.gl/maps/HAc2mfbV4yt
Phone :+64 4-801 5114
Address :192 Cuba St, Te Aro, Wellington 6141

The Larder Website
http://www.thelarder.co.nz/
The Larder Map
https://goo.gl/maps/9AYon3f2a9u
Phone :+64 4-891 0354
Address :133 Darlington Rd, Miramar, Wellington 6022

Matterhorn Website
http://matterhorn.co.nz/
Matterhorn Map
https://goo.gl/maps/6ZXCqEFV1ko
Phone :+64 4-384 3359
Address : 106 Cuba St, Te Aro, Wellington 6011

Hippopotamus Restaurant & Cocktail Bar
http://www.hippopotamus.co.nz/
Hippopotamus Restaurant & Cocktail Bar
https://goo.gl/maps/85azKrkQmp92
Phone :+64 4-802 8935
Address : Museum Hotel 90 Cable St, Te Aro,
Wellington 6011

Bars

Scotty and Mal's Website
http://www.scottyandmals.co.nz/
Scotty and Mal's Map
https://goo.gl/maps/75ruzeDPiyt
Phone :+64 4-802 5335
Address : 176 Cuba St, Wellington 6011

Motel Bar Website
http://motelbar.co.nz/
Motel Bar Map
https://goo.gl/maps/qmGhcyDCpcE2
Phone :+64 4-384 9084
Address :Forresters Ln, Te Aro, Wellington 6011

The Third Eye - Tuatara Website
http://tuatarabrewing.co.nz/the-third-eye/about
The Third Eye - Tuatara Map
https://goo.gl/maps/CGGttyYz7892
Address :30 Arthur St, Te Aro, Wellington 6011

Laundry Website
https://www.facebook.com/LaundryOnCuba
Laundry Map
https://goo.gl/maps/fpWoBYbMPmk
Phone :+64 4-384 4280
Address :242 Cuba St, Wellington 6011

Southern Cross Website
http://www.thecross.co.nz/
Southern Cross Bar Map
https://goo.gl/maps/MG2xAARHNw72
Phone :+64 4-384 9085
Address :39 Abel Smith St, Te Aro, Wellington 6011

C.G.R Merchant & Co. Website
http://www.cgrmerchant.co.nz/
C.G.R Merchant & Co. Map
https://goo.gl/maps/EnoskbfYVGw
Phone :+64 4-384 6737
Address :44 Courtenay Place, Te Aro, Wellington 6011

Meow Website
http://www.welovemeow.co.nz/
Meow Map
https://goo.gl/maps/1wqKVMUoSjG2
Phone :+64 4-385 8883
Address :9 Edward St, Te Aro, Wellington 6011

Hawthorn Lounge Website
http://www.hawthornlounge.co.nz/
Hawthorn Lounge Map
https://goo.gl/maps/azyb5GGxZx22
Phone :+64 4-890 3724
Address :82 Tory St, Te Aro, Wellington 6011

15

Wairarapa

Located in the southeastern part of North Island just an hour's drive from Wellington, the region of **Wairarapa** is known for its beautiful scenery and established vineyards.

Wairarapa Website
http://www.wairarapanz.com/
Wairarapa Map

https://goo.gl/maps/AY5b4cmQaCE2

If coming via Wellington, you will drive through the **Rimutaka Hill Road**; at the halfway point you see the region open up before you like a page from a fairytale book, with flat plains before you, a dramatic coastline to the east and rugged ranges covered in bush to the west.

Rimutaka Hill Road Map
https://goo.gl/maps/axrYhHudJU72

Wairarapa enjoys an atmosphere very different from other regions; it has a far more relaxed and chilled-out vibe. There are several cities and towns in Wairarapa that are well worth visiting, along with numerous natural and man-made attractions and experiences. Popular choices include hiking up **Waiohine Gorge** where you cross over a daring swing bridge that leads you to hiking tracks into the Tararuas, and visiting the quaint fishing town of **Ngawi** on the Cape Palliser coast where you can see numerous colorful tractors and bulldozers sitting on the shore.

Make time to explore several of the towns and cities in the Wairarapa region, each one boasting their own charms.

Waiohine Gorge Website
http://www.wairarapanz.com/see-and-do
/waiohine-gorge
Waiohine Gorge Map
https://goo.gl/maps/GhFAB8equk72

Ngawi Website
http://www.wairarapanz.com/ngawi
Ngawi Map
https://goo.gl/maps/Azrbm4hYztH2

Martinborough

The town of Martinborough is a popular stop through Wairarapa, particularly since boasts a colonial-era appeal and more than 30 wineries. The majority of these wineries is family-owned and can be found a stone's throw away from the town's square. A number of old buildings can be found within the area surrounding the square, along with numerous boutiques and restaurants serving locally sourced ingredients.

Martinborough Website
http://martinborough.com/
Martinborough Map
https://goo.gl/maps/VqWWVvAauJz

The **Martinborough Wine Center** offers guided sampling tours of the best wines produced in the region. You can even buy wine here, and they will ship it back to your home, so you don't have to take it back on the plane!

Martinborough Wine Center Website
http://www.martinboroughwinemerchants.com/
Martinborough Wine Center Map
https://goo.gl/maps/Uge5NDnbWck
Phone :+64 6-306 9040
Address :6 Kitchener St, Martinborough 5711

In November each year, the city hosts the Toast Martinborough festival, where visitors can enjoy food, wine, and music in a fantastically flamboyant atmosphere.

Greytown

If you are searching for that elusive, quaint little village reminiscent of a traditional Victorian countryside village, then look no further than Greytown. Founded in the mid-19th century, Greytown was the first town to be founded inland and has recently undergone a stylish transformation, making it a popular stop within Wairarapa.

Greytown Website
http://www.greytown.com/
Greytown Map
https://goo.gl/maps/vBeupEaBk8w

Visitors will enjoy wandering around Main Street with its range of stylish boutique stores, galleries, antique shops and restaurants, making it one of the best shopping experiences in the country.

Some of the best attractions in Greytown include Schoc Chocolate and The French Baker, two of the best food shops. Main Street is full of beautiful Victorian-era buildings, a beautiful example of old architecture. When you need a bigger dose of history, head to **Papawai Marae.** This is where the very first Maori Parliament was established and the traditional meetinghouse, known as a wharenui, was constructed in 1888. To understand more about early settler life, pay a visit to the Early Settlers Museum, which takes you on a fascinating history of the town's pioneers.

Papawai Marae Website
http://www.papawai.org.nz/
Papawai Marae Map
https://goo.gl/maps/gQTGg5Xkkd82
Phone :+64 6-304 9440

For nature lovers, you can see some rare animals at the **Pukaha Mount Bruce National Wildlife Center.** It is here that some of the country's rarest animals are bred and then released back into the wild. It is also home to the rarest kiwis - two white kiwis named Manukura and Mauriora - that are the pin-up poster creatures for the centers continuing conservation and educational programs. But the white kiwis are not the only beautiful creatures to see here; visitors can get up close with other rare birds including kokako, takahe and black teal, as well as watch wild kaka who come out of the forest to feed at 3pm.

Pukaha Mount Bruce National Wildlife Center Website
http://www.pukaha.org.nz/
Pukaha Mount Bruce National Wildlife Center Map
https://goo.gl/maps/doRv6HKBKwT2
Phone :+64 6-375 8004
Address :85379 SH 2, Mount Bruce 5881

Castlepoint Beach

Castlepoint Beach is a fun, family-friendly trip offering beautiful scenery and the opportunity to get to know the local culture and traditions. Climb up Castle Rock – all 162 meters of it – and gaze in wonder at the views of the surrounding area. Castlepoint Lighthouse is nearby and was one of the last lighthouses in the country to be erected. Pay a visit to Castlepoint Reserve, which houses the rare Brachyglottis Compactus, also known as the Castlepoint Daisy. The waters around the beach are frequently visited by New Zealand fur seals, dolphins and sometimes, even whales.

Castlepoint Beach Website
http://www.castlepoint.co.nz/
Castlepoint Beach Map
https://goo.gl/maps/cF74iskk8Zu

Cape Palliser
Located at the southernmost tip of North Island, **Cape Pelliser** is a short drive away from Wellington. An area of outstanding natural beauty, there are many attractions designed to entertain and amaze all who venture here.

Cape Palliser Website
http://www.wairarapanz.com/cape-palliser
Cape Palliser Map
https://goo.gl/maps/qYV1oGGX7Gy

Some of the best attractions include the Putangirua Pinnacles Scenic reserve, where you can see some strange-looking rocks and hike through the beautiful forest; the fishing village of Ngawi is not just oozing charm and appeal, but is home to the quirky tractors and bulldozers which line the shores; walk up the 250 steps of the Cape Pelliser Lighthouse and reward yourself with beautiful views over the ocean.

16

PART 2 - SOUTH ISLAND

Around 70% of New Zealand residents live on North Island, but on the South Island, you will discover a different side of the country. This part of New Zealand is much purer – it is a land which boasts landscapes that seem untouched by humans, home to a vast range of flora and fauna, making it one of the most spectacular places you could ever visit.

But there is so much more to the South Island than just scenery. The island boasts elite wineries, glacial valleys and a number of towns and scenic spots well worth exploring.

South Island Map
https://goo.gl/maps/WFSDjbtvNsz

17

Nelson

Nelson sits at the northwest tip of South Island, popular with both kiwis and international visitors due to it being the sunniest part of the entire country. Here in Nelson, you will experience a wide range of landscapes, from soft sandy beaches, dramatic mountain ranges and ancient forests.

For a long time, Nelson has attracted many artists (perhaps due in part to its sunny weather?) and today there are nearly 400 artists that call Nelson home, including traditional Maori and modern artists. Many of these artists offer visitors the chance to come and explore their studios.

Nelson's beaches are well known as some of the best in the country. **Golden Bay** is extremely popular and is family friendly. Other great places to explore include a trip inland to visit the country's biggest freshwater springs in **Takaka**, as well as visiting the **Abel Tasman track**. This hike will take between three and five days to complete but the scenery is outstanding. Otherwise you can enjoy the scenery as you kayak around the coastline and view fur seals and the blue penguins, which call this area home.

If you want to isolate yourself in an eco-friendly luxury retreat for a few days, then go and visit **The Resurgence Luxury Eco Lodge**.This is a great place to relax totally and clear your mind.

Nelson Website
http://www.nelsonnz.com/
Nelson Map
https://goo.gl/maps/9CfkF7EVaGx

Golden Bay Website
http://www.goldenbaynz.co.nz/
Golden Bay Map
https://goo.gl/maps/JGrZRB6Nn8z

Takaka Map
https://goo.gl/maps/R4uKBsLVgPL2

Abel Tasman Track Website
https://www.abeltasman.co.nz/abel-tasman

-national-park/abel-tasman-coast-track/
Abel Tasman Track Map
https://goo.gl/maps/5bjk1jcc4EM2
Address :Abel Tasman Coast Track, Abel Tasman National
Park 7183

The Resurgence Luxury Eco Lodge Website
http://www.resurgence.co.nz/
The Resurgence Luxury Eco Lodge Map
https://goo.gl/maps/jyGt7Xm7tLm
Tel:+64 3-528 4664
Address :574 Riwaka Valley Rd, Motueka 7198

After all this exploration, why not sit back and enjoy a range of local wines produced in the wineries surrounding Nelson. **Nelson Bay scallops** are a local delicacy here, served in many of the restaurants found within the city.

Nelson Bay Restaurant Website
http://www.styxrestaurant.co.nz/
Nelson Bay Restaurant Map
https://goo.gl/maps/Jnvp4NW1KU72
Phone :+64 3-548 1075
Address :272 Wakefield Quay, Stepneyville, Nelson 7010

Artistic and Cultural Nelson

As previously mentioned, Nelson boasts a highly creative atmosphere. If you are interested in exploring this cultural side, then there are a number of galleries and studios you should visit before leaving. Start with **The Suter Te Aratoi o Whakatu**, an art gallery which houses several works by Sir Tosswill Woollaston, famous for being one of the earliest modern artists within the country.

The Suter, Te Aratoi o Whakatu Website
https://www.thesuter.org.nz/
The Suter, Te Aratoi o Whakatu Map
https://goo.gl/maps/GXJUFH95A4T2
Phone :+64 3-548 4699
Address :28 Halifax St E, Nelson 7010

The **Hoglund Art Glass** is another highly popular studio with international tourists, located within seven acres of gardens, and produces outstanding glass works which you can purchase onsite.

Located just minutes away from downtown Nelson, the **World of Wearable Art and Collectable Cars Museum** is a museum dedicated to classical cars and art which you can wear (hence the name).

The Hoglund Art Glass Website
https://www.hoglundartglass.com/
The Hoglund Art Glass Map

https://goo.gl/maps/YPtVjrUTSX42
Phone :+64 3-544 6500
Address :7081, 52 Lansdowne Rd, Appleby 7081

The World of Wearable Art and Collectable Cars Museum Website
http://www.wowcars.co.nz/
The World of Wearable Art and Collectable Cars Museum Map
https://goo.gl/maps/AhMwuoSo6wR2
Phone :+64 3-547 4573
Address :Cadillac Way, Nelson 7011

Many artists from Nelson and the surrounding region frequently hold stands in the Saturday Market. Come here in the morning and check out some of their works and the other items on sale here.

For those interested in learning more about the Maori, there are trips into the surrounding bushland where your guides teach you about **Rongoa Maori**, the traditional Maori natural medicines.

Rongoa Maori Website
https://www.facebook.com/Rongoa-Maori-Traditional
-Maori-Medicine-156091344419407/

The Nelson Provincial Museum is a great place to visit to learn more about those who settled in Nelson centuries earlier and the history of the region.

The Nelson Provincial Museum Website
http://www.nelsonmuseum.co.nz/
The Nelson Provincial Museum Map
https://goo.gl/maps/TurwHy8SfW52
Phone :+64 3-548 9588
Address :Cnr Trafalgar St and Hardy Street, Nelson 7040

Another highly popular trip is to take a trip across the waters sailing to the **Abel Tasman National Park**, ideal for all the family.

Abel Tasman National Park Website
https://www.abeltasman.co.nz/
Abel Tasman National Park Map
https://goo.gl/maps/8T3WPFtFm6r

Accommodation and Restaurants: The best hotel you can stay in is undoubtedly the Rutherford Hotel Nelson. Dine at the Monaco Kitchen for the best dining experience.

Rutherford Hotel Nelson Website
http://www.rutherfordhotel.nz/
Rutherford Hotel Nelson Map
https://goo.gl/maps/HnxKHej6qqE2
Tel:+64 3-548 2299
Address :27 Nile St W, Nelson 7010

Monaco Kitchen Website
http://www.tmk.co.nz/
Monaco Kitchen Map
https://goo.gl/maps/fjYVMBc3u192
Phone :+64 3-547 0792
Address :6 Point Rd, Monaco, Nelson 7011

Immerse Yourself in the National Parks

Within the vicinity of Nelson, there are three national parks to explore at your leisure. Each one boasts a different atmosphere and appearance, but all are outstandingly beautiful. Read on to discover the unique charms of each national park.

The Abel Tasman Coastal Track takes up to five days to complete, but this hiking trail is one of the most popular within the country. Visitors can take a guide or go on their own and can be undertaken anytime during the year. You can also explore the coastline by sea kayaking trips, which can take up to several days. You will find a range of accommodation throughout the trail.

The Abel Tasman Coastal Track Website
https://www.abeltasman.co.nz/abel-tasman-national-park/abel-tasman-coast-track/
The Abel Tasman Coastal Track Map
https://goo.gl/maps/KSGuUTBwL8y

The Kahurangi National Park allows visitors to explore a range of wildlife, including plant life. The Heaphy Track is the most popular trail through the park and can take between four a five days to complete. The scenery here is outstanding and was used as the backdrop for the

Lord of the Rings movies.

The Kahurangi National Park Website
http://www.nelsonnz.com/getting-here-and
-around/places-to-visit/kahurangi-national-park/
The Kahurangi National Park Map
https://goo.gl/maps/PSYjfjzdNmx

The Nelson Lakes National Park is encased by mountainous terrain, providing a scenic backdrop that can hardly be described. Walk along Lake Rotoiti before hiking up to Lake Angelus, admiring the beauty of the bush, which allows you to imagine what the country would have been like five centuries earlier.

The Nelson Lakes National Park Website
http://www.nelsonlakes.co.nz/activities/

The Nelson Lakes National Park Map
https://goo.gl/maps/az86KmcLPx32

Golden Bay

Golden Bay offers visitors to immerse themselves in stunning natural beauty even before getting there – before you arrive in Golden Bay you have to drive **Takaka Hill**, known as the Marble Mountain – which is extraordinarily beautiful.

Takaka Hill Website
http://www.goldenbaynz.co.nz/directory-motueka-to-takaka.html
Takaka Hill Map
https://goo.gl/maps/dx53vxtYUz62

There are a number of attractions in and around Golden Bay. Start with a trip to **Te Waikoropupu Springs**. These are the biggest fresh-water springs in the entire country and are situated within a historic gold working reserve home to ancient bushland. Next, a safari trip to Farewell Spit should be on the list of things to see. This is a bird sanctuary set in wetlands, and has gained international acclaim due to its significance. When you need to relax, head to Wharariki Beach, which boasts gigantic sand dunes and dramatic rock formations. The region surrounding Golden Bay is home to several wineries that offer tours. The best wines produced here are Chardonnay, Pinot Noir and Sauvignon Blanc.

Te Waikoropupu Springs Website
http://www.doc.govt.nz/parks-and-recreation/
places-to-go/nelson-tasman/places/takaka-area
/te-waikoropupu-springs/
Te Waikoropupu Springs Map
https://goo.gl/maps/d3VPF1h1AkC2
Phone :+64 3-546 9339

Address :Pupu Springs Rd, Takaka 7183

Other ideal experiences in Golden Bay include horse riding excursions by the beaches of Narahau and Wharariki.

Whilst Golden Bay is well known for its culinary delights, the best food to try is smoked seafood, the best of which can be enjoyed at the **smokehouse** at Mapua. Speaking of the best, there are a number of internationally acclaimed spa resorts in the area surrounding Golden Bay, ideal for visitors seeking a place where they can rest the soul and body.

Smokehouse at Mapua Website
http://www.smokehouse.co.nz/
Smokehouse at Mapua Map
https://goo.gl/maps/TfdKscENWb42
Phone :+64 3-540 2280
Address :6 Aranui Rd, Mapua 7005

18

Marlborough

Marlborough is the biggest vineyard region famous for its production of Sauvignon Blanc wine. Positioned at the top of South Island, Marlborough offers visitors great weather, attractions, and scenery.

Marlborough Website

https://marlboroughnz.com/
Marlborough Map
https://goo.gl/maps/Xwr8ZPScQkv

The climate in Marlborough boasts numerous hours of sunshine and mild climate that allows visitors to remain comfortable as they explore everything the region has to offer throughout the year. There is no best time to come to Marlborough – it's great all year round, and numerous shows and events are held here throughout the different seasons.

More than 40 wineries have been established in Marlborough alone and wine tours are a great way to learn about the history of wine production in the region. These tours can be conducted privately, with a third-party company or by yourself. Enjoy can also enjoy a wine tasting bicycle tour.

Marlborough Wine Tours Website
http://marlboroughwinetours.co.nz/
Marlborough Wine Tours Map
https://goo.gl/maps/RP2ibsaiZEq
Phone :+64 3-574 2889
Address :269 Queen Charlotte Dr, RD 1, Picton 7281

One of the best attractions in the Marlborough region is the **Marl-borough Sounds**. There are a number of companies offering cruises to the Sounds; you can hire a sea kayak and explore them by yourselves as well if you want. Here, you can swim with the dolphins, go diving or fish. For those who prefer to stay dry, you can go hiking along the **Queen Charlotte track**, which trails through the forests and offers outstanding vistas of the cliffs and picturesque coves.

Marlborough Sounds Website
http://www.marlboroughsounds.co.nz/
Marlborough Sounds Map
https://goo.gl/maps/bi4nbQSHJkR2

Another great experience here is to explore the Marlborough High Country as it spills into **Kaikoura**. Explore the pinkish salt lakes located at Lake Grasmere before going on to **Molesworth Station**, the biggest active farmstead in the entire country. There are a number of homesteads in the region where you can stay – this is a great way of experiencing the area.

Kaikoura Website
http://www.kaikoura.co.nz/
Kaikoura Map
https://goo.gl/maps/GAH0YHeMUE12

Molesworth Station Website
http://www.molesworth.co.nz/
molesworth_station_tours.htm
Molesworth Station map
https://goo.gl/maps/rj504kvRbEw
Phone :+64 274 351 955
Address :50 State Highway 63, Renwick 7204

History lovers will not be disappointed at the amount of museums and other cultural attractions on offer. The **Omaka Aviation Heritage Center** boasts a wonderful collection of planes and artifacts dating from WWI, and each town in Marlborough has their own museums that take you on a fascinating journey of the history of the area.

The Omaka Aviation Heritage Center Website
http://www.omaka.org.nz/planning-visit-omaka.htm
The Omaka Aviation Heritage Center Map
https://goo.gl/maps/iuDMNpAB1Mx
Phone :+64 3-579 1305
Address :79 Aerodrome Rd, Omaka, Blenheim 7272

For visitors who really want a taste of the Marlborough region, the Sunday Farmers Market is a feast for the senses. Some of the best produce grown here includes honey and game, or else you can go pick fruit at one of the many orchards – a great way of keeping kids healthy and busy. **The Taylor River Reserve** offers fishing and the cakes in the nearby café are to die for.

Taylor River Reserve Website
http://www.marlborough.govt.nz/Recreation/Parks-and-Reserves/Re-serves/Blenheim/Taylor-River-Reserve.aspx

Marlborough offers a variety of walking and bicycle trails to choose from, many of which go through the **Wither Hills Mountain Bike Park** and Whites Bay. The beach at Whites Bay offers family-friendly swimming and other water activities, as does nearby Robin Hodd Bat.

Why not kayak to Wairau Lagoon, close to where humans first started living in the country and the home to nearly 100 different types of birds? You can also get here on foot if you wish.

Wither Hills Mountain Bike Park Website
http://www.marlborough.govt.nz/About-Marlborough
/Walking-and-Biking/Tracks2Do/Wither-Hills
-Farm-Park.aspx

Wither Hills Mountain Bike Park Map
https://goo.gl/maps/Mr9yQ485zD92
Address :Wither Hills, Blenheim 7201

Picton ‑ the opening to the Queen Charlotte Sound

Nearly 1/5th of the country's coastline is made up of the Marlborough Sands, which contains the Queen Charlotte Track. The best to explore it is via the sea, especially since there are numerous coves and bays that make up the **Queen Charlotte Sound.**

Picton Website
http://www.visitpicton.co.nz/
Picton Map
https://goo.gl/maps/5wGxGpfmWur

The little town of **Picton** is located in the Queen Charlotte Sound, founded by settlers in the mid‑19th century. A number of the original buildings from its founding still stand close to the waterfront, providing the town with a charming atmosphere.

There are a number of experiences waiting for you in and around Picton. Go **riding** along the **Queen Charlotte Track on bike** – this is one of the country's greatest cycling tracks.

Queen Charlotte Track on Bike Website
http://www.qctrack.co.nz/on-the-track/walk-the-track/
Queen Charlotte Track on Bike Map
https://goo.gl/maps/vRR15QZZ6Qr
email:qctsecretary@qctrack.co.nz

Next, pay a visit to the **National Whale Center** to learn more about the history of whaling and the creatures themselves in the area, before heading to the **Picton Museum**. Here, you will gain an intriguing glimpse into the history of the area before the settlers arrived and were inhabited by the Maori. If you get the chance, take a trip to Edwin Fox, located in Picton Harbor – it is the ninth largest ship in the world.

Due to its close proximity to the sea, visitors have the opportunity to explore the coastline by sea, either via a cruise where you can explore some of the beautiful coves and the waterfront restaurants, or via sea kayak (with a group or on your own).

National Whale Center Website
http://aworldwithwhales.com/
National Whale Center Map
https://goo.gl/maps/hXHRGCxzmS42
Phone :64 (0)3 5737876
Address : Building 1, London Quay,Picton Foreshore

Picton Museum Website
http://www.pictonmuseum-newzealand.com/
Picton Museum Map
https://goo.gl/maps/C9agseib8Z32
Phone :+64 3-573 8283
Address : 9 London Quay, Picton

There are a few shipwrecks in the Marlborough Sounds that you can dive to; the Mikhail Lermontov is the most popular as well as being the largest shipwrecks in the world that are good for **divers**. It can be found in the waters just off Port Gore.

Marlborough Sounds Diving Website
http://www.godive.co.nz/dive_site_information.html
Marlborough Sounds Diving Map
https://goo.gl/maps/xP93V47qu2G2
Phone :+64 800 463 483
Address :66 Wellington St, Picton 7220

Havelock

The charming coastal village of Havelock is a popular destination for those exploring the Marlborough Sounds. Once a wealthy gold mining town, it has now become renowned for its Greenshell mussels along with being the entryway to the Pelorus, Mahau, and Kenepuru Sands.

Havelock Website
http://www.havelocknz.com/
Havelock Map
https://goo.gl/maps/FNKvQ3uitt92

Due to being famous for its Greenshell mussels, when you visit Havelock you must try them. There are several restaurants along the waterfront that serve them or else sample them on the Greenshell Mussel Cruise.

Adventure awaits you in and around Havelock. Explore the waters of the Marlborough Sounds by kayak or onboard the **Pelorus Mail Boat.**

Head out to **Canvastown,** an old gold mining town, with its beautiful historic buildings and charming atmosphere before seeing **Pelorus Bridge Reserve** and the beautiful **Rai Valley,** both steeped in natural beauty and a range of wildlife.

Pelorus Mail Boat Website
http://themailboat.co.nz/
Pelorus Mail Boat Map
https://goo.gl/maps/gxzcMfPrVTR2
Phone :+64 3-574 1088
Address :Havelock Marina 1, Havelock 7100

Canvastown Website
https://www.facebook.com/places/Things-to-do-in-Canvastown-New-Zealand/115074461839143/

Canvastown Map
https://goo.gl/maps/MSoMftiQB5r

Pelorus Bridge Reserve Map
https://goo.gl/maps/LsgDWRrxh8Q2

Rai Valley Map
https://goo.gl/maps/ARy9SR8S2nB2

Marlborough Sounds Kajak Website
http://www.marlboroughsounds.co.nz/sea-kayaking-
in-the-marlborough-sounds/
Phone : 0800 283 283

Learn more about the wildlife and the history of the Pelorus and the **Kenepuru Sounds** onboard one of the boat trips or simply indulge in a bit of snapper fishing.

Kenepuru Sounds Map
https://goo.gl/maps/ezVZuPQndkG2

If you want to make your blood pump then why not cycle along the **Nydia Track** starting at Kaiuma Bay and finishing at Tennyson Inlet. For experienced riders, it takes up to eight hours each way or two days on foot.

Nydia Track Website
http://www.onthetracklodge.nz/
Nydia Track Map
https://goo.gl/maps/ZcWdLtzxXu12

Nearly 20 kilometers west of Havelock is the **Pelorus Bridge** where a number of walking experiences will certainly leave a big impression.

As previously mentioned, **The Hobbit**: the Desolation of Smaug was filmed here in New Zealand; the iconic barrel scene was filmed in the waters not far from Havelock. If you want to experience it for yourself, you can hire a kayak and journey down the same waters.

Pelorus Bridge Reserve Map
https://goo.gl/maps/LsgDWRrxh8Q2

Barewood Garden, located within the Awatere Valley, is a more calming experience but it is certainly well worth it. Beautiful and charming, it was proclaimed as a garden of National Significance and a popular attraction.

Barewood Garden Website
http://www.barewoodgarden.co.nz/
Barewood Garden Map
https://goo.gl/maps/A7jxecT8Sxt
Phone : +64 3 575 7432
Address :140 Barewood Road , Seddon , Marlborough 7285

One of the best wineries in the region is **Yealands Estate**, which is also the most ecological winery in the world.

Yealands Estate Website
http://www.yealands.co.nz/
Yealands Estate Map
https://goo.gl/maps/dNJK5ufsf912
Phone : +64 3-575 7618
Address :Cnr Seaview and Reserve Roads, Seddon, Blenheim

For nature lovers, experience the beauty and splendor of the region as you walk along the **Cape Campbell, Awatere Tussock Tracks** or bike along Molesworth Road. Make sure you take photos of **Mount Tapuae- o-Uenuku**, which dominates the skyline and was once climbed by Sir Edmund Hillary.
Cape Campbell Website

http://www.capecampbelltrack.co.nz/
Cape Campbell Map
https://goo.gl/maps/tQoN3MvkVNF2

Awatere Tussock Track Website
http://www.tussocktrack.co.nz/
Awatere Tussock Track Map
https://goo.gl/maps/endUa5Bxsm82

Mount Tapuae-o-Uenuku Website
https://marlboroughnz.com/guides/walks/mt-tapuae-o-uenuku
Mount Tapuae-o-Uenuku Map
https://goo.gl/maps/ufNzuNPzCEs

19

West Coast

Known by locals as **Westland** or The Coast, the West Coast stretches along the western side of the South Island. This is the country's most sparsely populated region, rich in natural beauty with rivers, rainforests, glaciers, seals and national parks. West Coast is the place to go if you like to surround yourself with rugged beauty.

Westland Website
http://www.glaciercountry.co.nz/
Westland Map
https://goo.gl/maps/Smmpv1KUmin

Beautiful experiences await you in the West Coast region. **Fox Glacier and Franz Josef Glacier** are huge expanses of ice, stretching out across the horizon as far as the eye can see. They are located within the **Westland Tai Poutini National Park** and makes you imagine that you have stepped into the world of Disney's Frozen.

Fox Glacier Website
http://www.glaciercountry.co.nz/explore-our-regions
/fox-glacier/

Franz Josef Glacier Website
http://www.glaciercountry.co.nz/explore-our-regions
/franz-josef-glacier/

Westland Tai Poutini National Park Website
http://www.doc.govt.nz/parks-and-recreation/places
-to-go/west-coast/places/westland-tai-poutini-national-park/

Westland Tai Poutini National Park Backpackers Website
http://www.backpackerguide.nz/westland-tai-poutini-
national-park-guide-backpackers/

Westland Tai Poutini National Park Map
https://goo.gl/maps/oAADKXDwpGB2

Mount Aspiring National Park is known for its beautiful river valleys and the dramatic mountain ranges that look down upon vast stretches of rough country. This is the country's third largest national park, and is situated not far from the Paparoa National Park, known for its subterranean rivers and limestone cliffs covered in forests.

Mount Aspiring National Park Website
http://www.backpackerguide.nz/mt-aspiring-national
-park-guide-backpackers/
Mount Aspiring National Park Map
https://goo.gl/maps/NoJK2MX9vDM2

Animal lovers will certainly want to pay a visit to the **Cape Foulwind Seal Colony**. A colony of seals lives and breed here, and it's certainly enjoyable just watching them frolic on the shore and spotting them in the water.

Cape Foulwind Seal Colony Map
https://goo.gl/maps/Te2gZNhVokP2

The **Heaphy Track** is considered one of the Great Walks, taking you through a range of different landscapes, from rainforests to mountains to picture-perfect beaches.

Heaphy Track Website
http://heaphytrack.com/
Heaphy Track Map
https://goo.gl/maps/PFpDfKrUf7A2

Okarito is the perfect place to just relax. This is the country's biggest natural estuary and kayak trips in the lagoon are highly popular with visitors since verdant rainforest surrounds it, home to over 70 species of bird.

20

Canterbury

Also known as Waitaha in the Maori language, **Canterbury** runs from the ocean to the Alps, renowned for its contrast of plains and mountainous peaks. **Christchurch** is perhaps the most recognized city, a place full of history and style, restaurants, shops and nature, both man-made and natural. Canterbury, no matter where you go, will certainly keep you busy and enthralled.

Canterbury Website
http://www.christchurchnz.com/asia/
Canterbury Map
https://goo.gl/maps/wm8Qt39MEDM2

Christchurch

Christchurch is often referred to as a trendy city and it isn't hard to see why. The city is inundated with museums, art galleries, stores and restaurants, all designed to tell the history and character of this remarkable town. Let's look at some of the best attractions within Christchurch.

Christchurch Website
http://www.christchurchnz.com/asia/
Christchurch Map

https://goo.gl/maps/C7CvMZbEGgL2

Re:START is a shopping area close to Cashel Mall. It was constructed out of shipping containers and can't be missed. Inside, there is a range of national and international shops along with cafes, and more containers are added each year.

Re:START Website
http://www.restart.org.nz/
Re:START Map
https://goo.gl/maps/1UULpc7vu952

If traveling with children, there are some great places to take them. The **International Antarctic Center** gives visitors a fascinating insight into one of the coldest places on earth, especially with the interactive exhibition where you can feel what it is like to be in the middle of a blizzard there.

International Antarctic Center Website
http://www.iceberg.co.nz/
International Antarctic Center Map
https://goo.gl/maps/jFi5q6Bgz1P2
Phone :+64 3-357 0519
Address :38 Orchard Rd, Christchurch Airport, Christchurch 8052

The Canterbury Museum houses a fascinating collection of artifacts relating to the history of the region; have a picnic in **Hagley Park** before paying a visit to the Christchurch Botanic Gardens.

Canterbury Museum Website
http://www.canterburymuseum.com/
Canterbury Museum Map

https://goo.gl/maps/Lk5Q2PTudm32
Phone :+64 3-366 5000
Address :Rolleston Ave, Christchurch 8013

Hagley Park Map
https://goo.gl/maps/D2dVoZqniJ12
Address :14 Riccarton Avenue, Christchurch Central, Christchurch 8011

For boys who love their toys, the **Air Force Museum** houses an impressive collection of historical aircraft, art, and artifacts. If tanks are more your thing then head to Tanks For Everything where you are given the opportunity to drive real military tanks and other vehicles as well as guided tours and other events.

Air Force Museum Website
http://www.airforcemuseum.co.nz/
Air Force Museum Map
https://goo.gl/maps/tN6fzDUW3CB2
Phone :+64 3-343 9532
Address :45 Harvard Ave, Wigram, Christchurch 8140

There is no better way to experience Christchurch than on a double-decker open top bus with the **Hassle Free Discover Christchurch Tour**.

The Port Hills, which surround Christchurch, are perfect for hiking, cycling and driving. Head into the hills and gaze in wonder at the city, Lyttelton Harbor and the Canterbury Plains spread out before you. For hikers and cyclers, be sure to check out the city council's website before heading up into the Port Hills as weather conditions can cause certain trails to be temporarily closed for health and safety reasons.

Hassle Free Discover Christchurch Tour Website
http://www.hasslefreetours.co.nz/tours/discover-christchurch/

Hassle Free Discover Christchurch Tour Map
https://goo.gl/maps/QFLt9YLiWLw
Phone :+64 800 427 753
Address :36 Harris Cres, Papanui, Christchurch 8053

Take a trip to the **Willowbank Wildlife Reserve** where you can see
and learn more about the kiwis, the national bird, and other birds who
live in the region. Head to Orana Wildlife Park where you can learn
more about a wide variety of creatures both big and small in gorgeous
settings.

Willowbank Wildlife Reserve Website
http://www.willowbank.co.nz/
Willowbank Wildlife Reserve Map
https://goo.gl/maps/EN7sDVwdmYz
Phone :+64 3-359 6226
Address :60 Hussey Rd, Northwood, Christchurch 8051

Orana Wildlife Park Website
http://www.oranawildlifepark.co.nz/
Orana Wildlife Park Map
https://goo.gl/maps/E1Dt2HNAmxy
Phone :+64 3-359 7109
Address :793 Mcleans Island Rd, Mcleans Island,
Christchurch 8051

Hotels, Restaurants, and Bars
I have put together a list of the best Hotels, Cafes, Restaurants, and
Bars for you to visit in Christchurch.

Hotels
Heritage Christchurch Hotel Website
http://www.heritagehotels.co.nz/hotels/heritage-christchurch

Heritage Christchurch Hotel Map
https://goo.gl/maps/meqU8ddvzu92
Tel:+64 3-983 4800
Address :28-30 Cathedral Square, Christchurch Central,
Christchurch 8011

The George Website
http://www.thegeorge.com/
The George Map
https://goo.gl/maps/ZgdTiAYUP8D2
Tel:+64 3-379 4560
Address :50 Park Terrace, Christchurch Central,
Christchurch 8013

Vagabond Backpackers Website
http://vagabondhostel.co.nz/
Vagabond Backpackers Map
https://goo.gl/maps/WDBow4oWNf82
Tel:+64 3-379 9677
Address :232 Worcester St, Christchurch Central,
Christchurch 8011

Restaurants and Bars
Christchurch Tramway Restaurant Website
http://welcomeaboard.co.nz/christchurch-tram
/tram-restaurant/
Christchurch Tramway Restaurant Map
https://goo.gl/maps/p87GWZgttcr
Phone :+64 3-366 7830
Address :7 Tramway Ln, Christchurch Central,
Christchurch 8011

Tequila Mockingbird Website

https://www.facebook.com/tequilamockingbird.chch/
Tequila Mockingbird Map
https://goo.gl/maps/iaQaVCNMFYJ2
Phone :+64 3-365 8565
Address :98 Victoria St, Christchurch Central,
Christchurch 8013

King of Snake Website
http://www.kingofsnake.co.nz/
King of Snake Map
https://goo.gl/maps/9cAXN6rRwFA2
Phone :+64 3-365 7363
Address :145 Victoria St, Christchurch Central,
Christchurch 8013

Bealey's Speight's Ale House Website
http://bealeysalehouse.co.nz/
Bealey's Speight's Ale House Map
https://goo.gl/maps/99h3i5rQuLK2
Phone :+64 3-366 9958
Address :263 Bealey Ave, Christchurch Central,
Christchurch 8013

No.4 Bar and Restaurant Website
http://www.no4bar.co.nz/
No.4 Bar and Restaurant Map
https://goo.gl/maps/FbNGS9b5otj
Phone :+64 3-355 3720
Address :4 Mansfield Ave, St Albans,
Christchurch 8014

The Craic Irish Bar Website
http://www.thecraicirishbar.co.nz/

The Craic Irish Bar Map
https://goo.gl/maps/FBsTSt9g9JN2
Phone :+64 3-343 4657
Address :84 Riccarton Rd, Riccarton,
Christchurch 8011

Banks Peninsula

The volcanic island of Banks Peninsula was active around 10,000,000 years ago but today it is home to a thriving arts scene and wildlife of all kinds.

Banks Peninsula Website
http://www.christchurchnz.com/destinations/akaroa-and-banks-peninsula/
Banks Peninsula Map
https://goo.gl/maps/LubRAxAqoty

The town of **Akaroa** offers a charming French colonial atmosphere and well known for its artistic character. The food in Akaroa will certainly take your taste buds on a trip to paradise – signature dishes include freshly caught salmon, crayfish, and Canterbury lamb. But don't forget to take a cruise around Akaroa Harbor where you may catch a glimpse of the Hector's dolphin – the rarest species of dolphin in the country!

Akaroa Website
http://www.akaroa.com/
Akaroa Map
https://goo.gl/maps/KnTukZToHuB2

Akaroa Harbor Map
https://goo.gl/maps/vir1LwXuEpm

Lyttelton

Another great town on the Banks Peninsular is Lyttelton. The town suffered a great deal of damage due to the earthquake in 2011 but continues to offer a mixture of restaurants, shops, and a Sunday Market. Don't forget to drive to Governors Bay and see the chocolate culinary attraction known as She Chocolat.

Lyttelton Map

https://goo.gl/maps/XtEGZtgnYxt

The Waipara Wine Valley and Hanmer Springs

Make your way north of Christchurch and you will discover the beginning of the **Alpine Pacific Triangle Touring Route**. Known for its range of outdoor experiences, hot springs and gourmet delights, the Waipara Wine Valley, and **Hanmer Springs** is a great place to visit.

Alpine Pacific Triangle Touring Route Website

http://www.christchurchnz.com/getting-around/
road-trips/experience-the-alpine-pacific-triangle/

Waipara Wine Valley Website
http://www.waiparavalleynz.com/
Waipara Wine Valley Map
https://goo.gl/maps/HFxvkG5guE42

Hanmer Springs Map
https://goo.gl/maps/sqGWeGNMbZr

Some of the best experiences here include riding the **Weka Pass Railway**, a popular attraction, taking you from **Waipara to Waikari**. Rafting on the Waiau River is a great way of getting your blood pumping before heading to the Hanmer Springs Thermal Reserve where you can soothe those aching muscles in the warm thermal waters. The forest surrounding Hanmer Springs offers a range of hiking trails and a hydro slide. **The Hanmer Springs** Ski Area is perfect for those who enjoy skiing.

Weka Pass Railway Website
http://www.wekapassrailway.co.nz/
Weka Pass Railway Map
https://goo.gl/maps/fBaYGFm7G182
Phone :+64 800 935 272
Address :113 Glenmark Dr, Waipara 7483

Waikari Map
https://goo.gl/maps/RRiJbptZjGA2

Rafting Website
http://www.hiddenvalleys.co.nz/new-zealand
-rafting.html

Phone :+64 3 696 3560

Hanmer Springs Thermal Reserve Website
http://hanmersprings.co.nz/
Hanmer Springs Thermal Reserve Map
https://goo.gl/maps/5VFonYsfmv42
Phone :+64 3-315 0000
Address :42 Amuri Ave, Hanmer Springs 7334

Gore Bay offers visitors the opportunity to go trout and salmon fishing in crystal clear waters and Kaikoura is home to a wide variety of sea creatures including fur seals, dolphins, penguins and sperm whales. A number of boat companies offer a range of boat trips out on the waters so you can see these magnificent creatures for yourself. You can even go swimming with the fur seals in the Kaikoura Peninsula as well as swim with the dolphins.

Gore Bay Website
http://www.gorebaycamp.co.nz/
Gore Bay Map
https://goo.gl/maps/DnkjsmFjTE72

For avian lovers, there are a variety of bird watching tours in the area, home to a wide range of bird species including Albatross, Molly-Mawks, and Petrels. Seabird colonies can be spotted along the **Kaikoura Peninsular Walkway**, a three-hour return trip where you can also spot fur seals.

Kaikoura Peninsular Walkway Map
https://goo.gl/maps/PhGdWY88zFy

Mackenzie
Mackenzie is famous for its endless blue skies, blue lakes, and

mountainous ranges. Picture perfect, the area, is home to a variety of natural and historical attractions guaranteed to keep everyone entertained.

Mackenzie Website
http://mtcooknz.com/
Mackenzie Map
https://goo.gl/maps/rN1276Vt8aA2

Start your trip here by heading to the **Church of the Good Shepherd** by the banks of Lake Tekapo and then **charter a flight** from here or Glentanner Station to be taken up over the Southern Alps, the West Coast Glaciers, and the Aoraki Mount Cook for outstanding vistas.

For adrenaline junkies, take a ski plane and set down on the Tasman Glacier or you can go heli-skiing through the serene alpine region. Tubing is offered at **Tekapo Springs**; it is also open during the summer months so can be enjoyed all throughout the year. But if you want to simply relax then sink beneath the waters of the hot pools and bask in the glorious views of the lake.

Church of the Good Shepherd Website
http://www.mackenziechurch.org.nz/
Church of the Good Shepherd Map
https://goo.gl/maps/HmNGstDRZ9J2
Phone :+64 3-685 8389

Flight Charter Website
http://mtcooknz.com/tours/air-safaris/
Phone :+64274748687

Tekapo Springs Website
http://www.tekaposprings.co.nz/
Tekapo Springs Map
https://goo.gl/maps/x5mtCXoh84S2
Phone :+64 3-680 6550
Address :6 Lakeside Dr, Lake Tekapo 7945

Mount Cook Alpine Salmon Farm is situated between Lake Tekapo and **Aoraki Mount Cok National Park** and offers visitors the chance to learn why the salmon here is considered to be one of the best – you can even sample Saikou Sushi salmon!

Mount Cook Alpine Salmon Farm Website
http://alpinesalmon.co.nz/
Mount Cook Alpine Salmon Farm Map
https://goo.gl/maps/RgHdAruieVM2
Phone :+64 3-435 0427
Address :Lake Pukaki Information Centre, SH8,
between Tekapo and Twizel, Pukaki 7999

Aoraki Mount Cok National Park Map
https://goo.gl/maps/ZYHzDNQnaAF2
Phone :+64 3-435 1186

The Mackenzie Basin is the ideal place for lovers at night. The basin was recently proclaimed as the biggest International **Dark Sky Reserve**, Gaze up into the velvet darkness of the sky and be amazed at the sheer brilliance of the stars shining down.

International Dark Sky Reserve Website

http://darksky.org/idsp/reserves/aorakimackenzie/

There are a number of hiking trails on offer at Aoraki Mount Cook National Park, home to the Mount Cook Lily.

For history lovers, Canterbury certainly won't disappoint. Take a drive to Raincliff to see the biggest collection of Maori Rock Art in the entire country and Timaru boasts an extraordinary collection of Victorian and Edwardian era architecture.

You cannot leave the region without seeing the film location of Edoras, which was the fortress of the Rohan people in **The Lord of the Rings** movies.

The Lord of the Rings Location Tours Website
http://www.hasslefreetours.co.nz/tours/lord-of-the-rings
Phone :+64 3 385 5775

If traveling with teens, go rafting down the **Rangitata River**, which boasts grade five rapids. For parents, there are great wine tours to participate on in Opihi, which also offer lunches.

Rangitata River Rafting Website
http://www.rafts.co.nz/
Phone : 0800 251 251
Address :Peel Forest ,RD205 ,South Canterbury

Opihi Wine Website
http://www.winesofnz.com/winery/opihi-vineyards/
Opihi Wine Map
https://goo.gl/maps/gyi9xqEXdTH2
Phone : +64 3-614 8308
Address :804 Opihi Rd, Pleasant Point 7982

In the middle of the Canterbury region, between the Southern Alps and Christchurch, you will discover a different side of the area. Visitors can enjoy a spot of river fishing, with the **Rakaia River** famous for salmon between February and March.

Rakaia River Map
https://goo.gl/maps/MB7XvwHh8N32

While the Oriental Express may be the best train ride in the world, the **TranzAlpine Express** here in Canterbury certainly makes the top six. Gaze out at the beauty of the region as you make your way to Arthur's Pass, where you can go hiking and explore waterfalls.

TranzAlpine Express Website
http://www.kiwirailscenic.co.nz/tranzalpine/
TranzAlpine Express Map
https://goo.gl/maps/kRd227Rhev12
Phone : +64 4-495 0775
Address :Troup Dr, Addington, Christchurch 8011

Other great things to do here include enjoying a spot of golf at the base of the Southern Alps, going on an eco-tour to learn more about the rare creatures and plant life in the area or go skiing at **Mount Hutt**, boasting the longest ski season in this part of the world.

Mount Hutt Website
https://www.nzski.com/mt-hutt
Mount Hutt Map
https://goo.gl/maps/KyNjPvY3t6P2
Phone : +64 3 308 5074
Address :Mt Hutt Skifield Access Road,
Mount Hutt 7782

21

Waitaki

The **Waitaki** region in South Island is a beautiful blend of outstanding natural beauty and charming coastline, scattered with rich Maori historical attractions and quaint towns.

Waitaki Website
http://www.visitoamaru.co.nz/visit/waitaki-valley.aspx
Waitaki Map

https://goo.gl/maps/HjmWV19XSU32

If visiting the Waitaki region, then here are some of the best things to see and experience.

Perfect for children and adults alike, head to the town of **Palmerston** and go horse riding at **Springbank Farms** or perhaps go cycling part of the way along the Alps 2 Ocean trail. Marvel at the amount of blue penguins heading to the beach at the **Oamaru Blue Penguin colony**.

Palmerston Map
https://goo.gl/maps/3vMnfd4SeAC2

Springbank Farm Website
http://springbankfarm.co.nz/
Springbank Farm Map
https://goo.gl/maps/tRRCvMjYH8C2
Phone : +64 3-465 1223
Address :2 R.D. Palmerston, Otago, Palmerston 9061

Oamaru Blue Penguin Colony Website
http://www.penguins.co.nz/
Oamaru Blue Penguin Colony Map

https://goo.gl/maps/UeUMHFxtss32
Phone : +64 3-433 1195
Address :Waterfront Rd, Oamaru 9400

Culture lovers will fall head over heels at the **Moeraki Boulders** –
perfectly round, they continue to be a mystery even today. Visit the Te
Ana Maori Rock Art Center, the largest Maori rock art in the country,
before heading to Totara Estate where you can learn about the early
history of the country's farming industry. The Vanished World Center
in Duntroon is great for understanding about the prehistory of New
Zealand, with their own fossil trails.

Moeraki Boulders Website
http://www.moerakiboulders.com/

Moeraki Boulders Map
https://goo.gl/maps/iXQp336S2vz
Phone : +64 3-439 4827
Address :7 Moeraki Boulders Rd, Hampden 9482

Still want more? There are a number of quaint towns and villages that shouldn't be passed up on. The fishing village of **Moeraki** oozes charm and the fresh seafood is well worth waiting for. **Oamaru** is another charming town with a picture-perfect harbor, Victorian-era stores and historical buildings featuring Oamaru Whitestone. When you need to relax a little more (and why not?) then head to the Hot Tubs Omarama or **Ladybird Hill**, which is the highest winery in New Zealand.

Moeraki Website
http://www.moerakivillageholidaypark.co.nz/
Moeraki Map
https://goo.gl/maps/5hG5aQvWaa72

Oamaru Website
http://www.visitoamaru.co.nz/home.aspx
Oamaru Map
https://goo.gl/maps/qPbL17mNK9q

Hot Tubs Omarama Website
http://www.hottubsomarama.co.nz/
Hot Tubs Omarama
https://goo.gl/maps/ALP2Pr4wNnr
Phone : +64 3-434 8115
Address :468 Beach Rd, Oamaru 9495

Ladybird Hill Website
http://www.ladybirdhill.co.nz/

Ladybird Hill Map
https://goo.gl/maps/Finz564Ht3G2
Phone : +64 3-438 9550
Address :1 Pinot Noir Ct, Omarama 9412

22

Otago

The South-Eastern Region of New Zealand is **Otago**.The Otago area is another region in this amazing country with breathtaking natural beauty.In Otago, you will find a wide variety of contrasting areas for you to enjoy.Otago has sandy beaches, snowy mountains, and glacial lakes.

Otago Website 1

http://www.otago.co.nz/
Otago Website 2
http://www.centralotagonz.com/
Otago Map
https://goo.gl/maps/wfymT8vCE9o

Dunedin

Dunedin is the biggest city in Otago and is a city filled with culture and history.Visiting Dunedin is always fun, and you will find a wide variety of activities.

Dunedin Website 1
https://www.dunedinnz.com/visit
Dunedin Website 2
http://www.insidersdunedin.co.nz/attractions-insider
Dunedin Map

https://goo.gl/maps/r5Cuhnpeo4J2

For art lovers check out **Gallery De Novo**.After that, you can spend a few hours in the **Otago Museum**.

Gallery De Novo Website
http://www.gallerydenovo.co.nz/
Gallery De Novo Map
https://goo.gl/maps/b7rZie67Fd32
Phone : +64 3-474 9200
Address :101 Stuart St, Dunedin, 9016

Otago Museum Website
http://otagomuseum.nz/
Otago Museum Map
https://goo.gl/maps/Br43UXfBvC62
Phone : +64 3-474 7474
Address :419 Great King St, North Dunedin, Dunedin 9016

Dunedin is a coastal city with many beaches on its coastline.If you have time check out **Allans Beach**.

Allans Beach Website
http://www.outsideonline.com/1859296
/top-10-new-zealand-beaches#slide-8
Allans Beach Map
https://goo.gl/maps/7xTiAyyUr7n

New Zealand is famous for their National Rugby Team the **All Blacks,** and Otago is famous for their Regional Rugby Team the **Otago Highlanders**.If you are a sports enthusiast, then go and check out the **Dunedin Rugby Stadium**.If you are there in the winter, then go and enjoy a Super Rugby match.

All Blacks Website
http://www.allblacks.com/

Otago Highlanders Website
http://thehighlanders.co.nz/

Dunedin Rugby Stadium Website
http://www.forsythbarrstadium.co.nz/
Dunedin Rugby Stadium Map
https://goo.gl/maps/2HweZGWE4tA2
Phone : +64 3-479 2823
Address :130 Anzac Ave, Dunedin 9058

Hotels, Restaurants, and Bars
I have put together a list of the best Hotels, Cafes, Restaurants, and Bars for you to visit in Dunedin

Hotels
Hotel St Clair Website
http://www.hotelstclair.com/
Hotel St Clair Map
https://goo.gl/maps/FHyZcH5DKxn
Tel:+64 3-456 0555
Address :24 Esplanade, St Clair, Dunedin 9012

Amross Motel Website
http://www.amrossmotel.co.nz/
Amross Motel Map
https://goo.gl/maps/RvpfrfXso9M2
Tel:+64 3-471 8924
Address :660 George St, North Dunedin, Dunedin 9016

Larnach Castle Website
http://www.larnachcastle.co.nz/Accommodation
-at-Larnach-Castle
Larnach Castle Map

https://goo.gl/maps/xQxNsKbfh2x
Tel:+64 3-476 1616
Address :145 Camp Rd, Dunedin 9077

Dunedin Holiday Park and Motels Website
http://dunedinholidaypark.co.nz/
Dunedin Holiday Park and Motels Map
https://goo.gl/maps/Vc2Z9e1GGyv
Tel:+64 3-455 4690
Address :41 Victoria Road, St Kilda, Dunedin 9012

Restaurants
Two Chefs Bistro Website
http://twochefsbistro.com/
Two Chefs Bistro Map
https://goo.gl/maps/vqR91tiizbz
Phone :+64 3-477 7293
Address :121 Stuart St, Dunedin, 9016

Scotia Bar and Bistro Website
http://www.scotiadunedin.co.nz/
Scotia Bar and Bistro Map
https://goo.gl/maps/Nqc5CmvuuX52
Phone :+64 3-477 7704
Address :199 Stuart St, Dunedin, 9016

Esplanade Website
http://www.esplanade.co/
Esplanade Map
https://goo.gl/maps/4btSEho8pYE2
Phone :+64 3-456 2544
Address :250 Forbury Rd, Otago 9012

Ironic Cafe & Bar Website
http://www.ironiccafebar.co.nz/
Ironic Cafe & Bar Map
https://goo.gl/maps/7GJYxGqYRr72
Phone :+64 3-477 9988
Address :9 Anzac Ave, Dunedin 9016

Bars
Inch Bar Website
https://www.facebook.com/Inch-Bar-100507150007389/
Inch Bar Map
https://goo.gl/maps/cnHNCBNSrjP2
Phone :+64 3-473 6496
Address :8 Bank St, Otago 9010

Speights Ale House Website
http://www.thealehouse.co.nz/
Speights Ale House Map
https://goo.gl/maps/8zacfopXx032
Phone :+64 3-471 9050
Address :200 Rattray St, Dunedin, 9016

Tonic Website
http://www.tonicbar.co.nz/
Tonic Map
https://goo.gl/maps/6zwKeCKjk6U2
Phone :+64 3-471 9194
Address :138 Princes St, Dunedin, 9016

Stuart St Mac's Brew Bar Website
http://www.stuartst.co.nz/
Stuart St Mac's Brew Bar Map

https://goo.gl/maps/J9LUCitPeEq
Phone :+64 3-477 3776
Address :Ground Floor, 12 The Octagon, Dunedin, 9010

Queenstown

Queenstown is probably one of the most famous towns in New Zealand.The Town is built around Lake Wakatipu, and it has amazing views over the mountains.Queenstown is one of the best places in the country.It's absolutely gorgeous and has just the right mix of adventure and relaxation.If I could only visit one city in New Zealand, then Queenstown would be my choice.

Queenstown Website 1
http://www.queenstownnz.co.nz/
Queenstown Map
https://goo.gl/maps/qqwoLjMkMPn

Queenstown is the unofficial adventure capital of New Zealand and is known as a resort town.If you are the outdoors type, then you will love Queenstown.Activities include **Jet Boating, mountain biking, tramping, paragliding, skydiving, white water rafting,bungy jumping, skiing, and snowboarding**.If you are not into the adrenaline activities, then go fly-fishing by the lake.

Queenstown has become one of the more trendy towns in New Zealand and attracts a wide variety of people that are not into adventure sports.Queenstown has some **fine restaurants** and bars and people come from all over the New Zealand and the world to enjoy this town.

Jet Boating Website
http://www.shotoverjet.com/
Jet Boating Map
https://goo.gl/maps/t6VLi1nS4c22
Phone :+64 3-442 8570
Address :Gorge Rd, Queenstown 9300

Mountain Biking Website
http://vertigobikes.co.nz/
Mountain Biking Map
https://goo.gl/maps/RkABJYcdFGB2
Phone :+64 3-442 8378
Address :4 Brecon St, Queenstown 9300

Tramping Website
http://www.queenstownnz.co.nz/information/

walking-hiking/

Paragliding Website
http://www.nzgforce.com/
Paragliding Map
https://goo.gl/maps/WP4HfDXoYXB2
Phone :+64 800 759 688

Skydiving Website
http://www.nzoneskydive.co.nz/home
Skydiving Map
https://goo.gl/maps/fTTDhEdmjx42
Phone :+64 3-442 5867
Address :35 Shotover St, Queenstown 9300

White Water Rafting Website
http://www.queenstownrafting.co.nz/
White Water Rafting Map
https://goo.gl/maps/eexGmCMJtXw
Phone :+64 3-442 9792
Address :35 Shotover St, Queenstown Town 9300

Bungy Jumping Website
http://www.bungy.co.nz/
Bungy Jumping Map
https://goo.gl/maps/cHXJADWo7U12
Phone :+64 3-450 1300
Address :25 Shotover St Crn of Shotover and, Camp St,
Queenstown 9300

Skiing and Snowboarding Website
http://www.queenstownnz.co.nz/information
/winter-sports/

Queenstown Website 2
https://www.everythingqueenstown.com/

Hotels, Restaurants, and Bars
I have put together a list of the best Hotels, Restaurants, and Bars for you to visit in Queenstown.

Hotels
Villa del Lago Website
http://www.villadellago.co.nz/
Villa del Lago Map
https://goo.gl/maps/7vvwi8teW6P2
Tel:+64 3-442 5727
Address :249 Frankton Rd, Queenstown 9300

The Spire Hotel Website
http://www.thespirehotel.com/
The Spire Hotel Map
https://goo.gl/maps/ve1KWqCDQ2T2
Tel:+64 3-441 0004
Address:3-5 Church Lane, Queenstown 9300

Canyons Lodge Website
http://www.thecanyonslodge.com/
Canyons Lodge MAddress:ap
https://goo.gl/maps/reXWF3P1kD12
Tel:+64 3-442 6108
13 Watties Track, Arthurs Point 9371

Arrowtown House Boutique Hotel
http://www.arrowtownhouse.com/
Arrowtown House Boutique Hotel
https://goo.gl/maps/wBceBHbzxzA2

Tel:+64 3-441 6008
Address :10 Caernarvon St, Arrowtown 9302

Haka Lodge Website
http://www.hakalodge.com/lodges/haka-lodge-queenstown/
Haka Lodge Map
https://goo.gl/maps/TPo5PFJcbk62
Tel:+64 3-442 4970
Address :6 Henry St, Queenstown 9300

Restaurants
Skyline Website
http://www.skyline.co.nz/queenstown/restaurant/
Skyline Map
https://goo.gl/maps/tkcnP88Q2HA2
Phone :+64 3-441 0101
Address :Brecon St, Queenstown 9300

The Bathhouse Website
http://www.bathhouse.co.nz/
The Bathhouse Map
https://goo.gl/maps/e5mg9UBMeXT2
Phone :+64 3-442 5625
Address :38 Marine Parade, Queenstown Town Centre 9300

Winnies Website
http://www.winnies.co.nz/
Winnies Map
https://goo.gl/maps/5PJwifKrWvv
Phone :+64 3-442 8635
Address :7-9 The Mall, Queenstown 9348

Botswana Butchery Website
http://www.botswanabutchery.co.nz/
Botswana Butchery Map
https://goo.gl/maps/hARqw4JR7Mu
Phone :+64 3-442 6994
Address :17 Marine Parade, Queenstown East 9300

Bars
Cowboy Qt Ltd Website
https://www.facebook.com/pages/Cowboys
/147691695293157
Cowboy Qt Ltd Map
https://goo.gl/maps/f2etqxecKoM2
Phone :+64 3-409 2978
Address :7 Searle Ln, Queenstown 9300

Atlas Beer Cafe Website
http://atlasbeercafe.com/
Atlas Beer Cafe Map
https://goo.gl/maps/5YEpGzXYztL2
Phone :+64 3-442 5995
Address :Steamer Wharf, 88 Beach Street, Queenstown Town
Centre 9300

Threesixty Restaurant & Bar Website
https://www.facebook.com/pages/Threesixty
-Restaurant/229178517095505
Threesixty Restaurant & Bar Map
https://goo.gl/maps/21Quukd8NBo
Phone :+64 3-442 5360
Address :93 Beach Street, Town Centre 9300

Bar Up Website

http://www.barup.co.nz/
Phone :+64 3-442 7067
Address :Corner of Searle Lane & Eureka Arcade

23

Southland

Southland

New Zealand's southernmost region is Southland.It is also the area in New Zealand's with the smallest population in the country.However if you are interested in seeing even more beautiful scenery then take a trip down to Southland.If you are lucky, you might see the mysterious Kiwi bird in the stunning landscapes of Southland.

Southland Website
http://www.southlandnz.com/
Southland Map
https://goo.gl/maps/WzFE1fJkfM92

Invercargill

Invercargill is the "capital" of Southland and is also home to the local government.Invercargill is the world's southernmost city, and this little city will surprise you with what it has to offer.

Take a walk to the **Southland museum** and art gallery and learn about this fascinating part of New Zealand.If Museums are not your thing, then take the 10 kilometer trip to **Oreti Beach**. Oreti Beach stretches for 26 kilometers.Want to clear your mind and take the longest beach walk of your life?Then this is the beach for you.

Invercargill Website
http://www.invercargillnz.com/
Invercargill Map
https://goo.gl/maps/6Hdg4CH2rLF2

Southland and Art Gallery Website

http://southlandmuseum.co.nz/
Southland and Art Gallery Map
https://goo.gl/maps/fRU2QV5iNBv
Phone :+64 3-219 9069
Address :108 Gala St, Invercargill 9810

Oreti Beach Website
http://www.nzsurfguide.co.nz/surf_breaks/southland
/oreti-beach
Oreti Beach Map
https://goo.gl/maps/uYKUGSx5dez

National Parks
Southland is home to two national parks.The parks are Fiordland National Park and Rakiura National Park.Rakiura National Park is on Stewart Island. Stewart Island is part of the Southland area and is located 30 kilometers south of the South Island of New Zeland.

The Fiordland National Park is home to the highest waterfall in New Zeland, the Brown Falls.

The Fiordland National Park Website
http://www.fiordland.org.nz/about-fiordland
/fiordland-national-park/
The Fiordland National Park Map
https://goo.gl/maps/BypoVwXCdsN2

Brown Falls Map
https://goo.gl/maps/HbDsj2rSJMN2

Rakiura National Park Website
http://www.stewartisland.co.nz/organisations/
information-and-bookings/rakiura-national-

park-visitor-centre/
Rakiura National Park Map
https://goo.gl/maps/Cz6Do7GgMSv

Stewart Island Website
http://www.stewartisland.co.nz/

Hotel Invercargill
Victoria Railway Hotel Website
http://www.hotelinvercargill.co.nz/
Victoria Railway Hotel Map
https://goo.gl/maps/bZpMnQSJ4Dz
Tel:+64 3-218 1281
Address :3 Leven St, Invercargill 9840

24

10 Unique Things to Do in New Zealand

New Zealand is a unique place to visit, and there are a number of things you can do here that you can't do anywhere else. Read on to discover the top ten unique things to do in this small country with a big personality (even though there are numerous other reasons to start booking your flights).

Unique Food
Due to its colonial history, New Zealand food has often been com-

pared with the traditional British Sunday roast (which usually consists of lamb, potatoes, and vegetables) but modern New Zealand cuisine is something completely different to what it was a few decades ago. The chefs in this country have found inspiration in a number of culinary delights and techniques, especially when it comes to seafood, and have created a fresh, tasty cuisine all of its own. Don't forget to try some traditional Maori cuisine – paua (abalone), sea urchins and kumara – dishes you will be hard to find anywhere else. And don't forget to sample the wines produced at the number of wineries in the country.

Unique Cultures

While the dramatic and diverse landscapes of New Zealand are completely breathtakingly beautiful, there is nowhere in the world where you can learn about the Maori people than by visiting them in their own country. The Maori are the descendants of the Pacific Ocean Islanders who settled in New Zealand several centuries ago and have still retained much of their traditions and culture today. Visitors can tour traditional Maori villages, participate in a Haka (a traditional Maori war dance), or eat at a hangi, a Maori feast. Learn how to create traditional Maori jewelry and crafts, learn about the mythology and legends surrounding places and people along rivers and mountains.

Unique Cultures Website
http://www.inz.maori.nz/

Unique Animal Life

Due to its located near to the bottom of the globe, New Zealand boasts a wide variety of different animals, many of which are native to these islands. Some of these animals include the tuatara, a reptile that is a close relation to the now extinct dinosaurs. The kiwi is the national bird; this small, flightless bird can be seen in its native habitat along with the kea, an alpine parrot native to the country. Other rare and native birds of New Zealand include the grand royal albatross and the yellow eyes penguin. The waters surrounding the islands include the rare Hectors dolphin and fur seals.

Find Fantasy Worlds

Numerous countries around the world claim to have the most dramatic scenery but New Zealand's diverse landscapes are worthy of filming. Wait, they already have been! New Zealand provided the rugged backdrop for the Lord of the Rings movies and The Hobbit: The Desolation of Smaug.

Driving to these locations is an adventure all on its own, driving through out-of-this-world landscapes in jeeps, helicopters and even on horseback. Dive into the world of fantasy at the sites of Edoras and the Plains of Rohan.

Lord of the Rings Tour Website
http://www.lordoftheringstours.co.nz/main.html
Phone :0800568759 (Free NZ)
+64212633318 (International)

Geothermal Wonders

While New Zealand is, by geological standards, a young country at under ten thousand years old, it boasts a staggering amount of geothermal wonders. Volcanic islands dot the coastline and geothermal sites through the middle of North Island. Thermal hot springs can be found throughout the country, especially at Taupo and Rotorua, with the smell of Sulphur in the air and mud pools boiling up, making it a completely different landscape to what you may imagine.

Volcanic Wonderland Website
http://www.waiotapu.co.nz/
Volcanic Wonderland Map
https://goo.gl/maps/tzr9GrPvyjq
Phone :+64 7-366 6333
Address :201 Waiotapu Loop Rd, Rotorua 3073

Whale Watching

New Zealand is famous for its whale watching safaris. There are some boat operators providing tours out into the ocean with highly trained and professional guides, introducing you to a variety of whales that swim close to the country. Many of these offer around 80% of the fee if you don't see any whales (95% of the trips are actually successful).

Whale Watching Website
http://www.whalewatch.co.nz/
Whale Watching Map
https://goo.gl/maps/u7XezMJFK2r
Phone :+64 3-319 6767
Address :The Whaleway Station Whaleway Road, Kaikoura 7340

Skywalk in Auckland

The Skywalk is a jaw-dropping, adrenaline pumping walk around the Sky Tower. Sounds innocent, right? The walk is located 192 meters up off the ground, and the walkway is 1.2 meters wide, and there are no rails to hold onto! But don't worry; you are fitted with a safety harness in case you miss your footing.

Skywalk in Auckland Map
https://goo.gl/maps/Sr1kBgBHCRN2
Phone :+64 9-368 1835
Address :72 Victoria St W, Auckland 1141

Walk Across a Glacier

Where else can you go and walk across a glacier? You can in New Zealand. There are a few companies that offer small group tours with professional guides and all gear supplied. You arrive and depart by helicopter, taking around five minutes, and you spend the next three hours on the actual glacier. Another tour will take you higher up the glacier; the flights take around ten minutes, and you get two hours on the glacier.

Glacier Website
http://www.glaciercountry.co.nz/

Jump From a Plane

New Zealand is often visited for its vast range of outdoor activities and experiences. Skydiving is a highly enjoyable, blood pumping experience, guaranteed to get your heart racing. New Zealand offers numerous places where you can go skydiving, but Taupo is the best – and most popular – place to jump.

Taupo Skydiving Website
http://www.skydivetaupo.co.nz/
Taupo Skydiving Map
https://goo.gl/maps/z2jEdwZBKZT2

Phone :+64 7-377 8300
Address :1465 Anzac Memorial Dr, Wharewaka,
Taupo 3378

Go Skiing in Summer

Usually, you have to wait until winter to go skiing in most countries but no, not in New Zealand. In this country, due to its seasons, you can go skiing between June and October. Many hiking trails on mountainous slopes are transformed into the perfect skiing terrain with numerous luxury resorts providing a comfortable base. Don't forget to try heli-skiing, where a helicopter takes you up to remote terrain and experience outstanding ski runs that you won't find anywhere else.

Heli-Skiing Website
http://www.heliski.co.nz/heliski-and-heliboard
-new-zealand-queenstown-wanaka-mt-cook/
Heli-Skiing Map
https://goo.gl/maps/NuzwTXb7dBP2
Phone :+64 3-442 6722
Address :The Station Building, Cnr Shotover
and Camp Streets, Queenstown 9300

25

Conclusion

I want to thank you for reading this book! I sincerely hope that you received value from it . I hope you now have a better idea of what New Zealand has to offer.